| DATE | | |
|---|---|---|
| | | |
| | | |
| | | |
| | | |
| | | |
| | | |
| | | |
| | | |
| | | |
| | | |
| | | |
| | | |
| | | |

# EPIGRAMS FROM MARTIAL

MARCUS VALERIUS MARTIALIS.

# EPIGRAMS FROM MARTIAL
A Verse Translation
by Barriss Mills

Purdue University Studies
Lafayette, Indiana

iii

Acknowledgment is due to Walter C.
A. Ker, editor, and to the Loeb Classical
Library and Harvard University Press,
publishers, for the Latin text of epigram
I, i, taken from Martial, *Epigrams*, Vol.
I, p. 30.

# CONTENTS

# PREFACE

In making these translations I have followed the Loeb's text of Martial, edited by Walter C. A. Ker, except in a few places where I have preferred an alternate reading offered by Ker himself or by H. M. Stephenson in his *Selected Epigrams of Martial.* Stephenson's notes have helped me through the occasional difficulties in Martial's Latin, and I could scarcely have attempted my own versions of the epigrams without the translations of Ker, Pott and Wright, Francis and Tatum, and "M. S. B.," the modest author of an unexpurgated, literal prose rendering "privately printed" in 1921. I wish to thank Daniel J. Kaufman and his mother, Mrs. Ruth Lyons Kaufman, for lending me their copy of that little-known book—the only one I have seen which has the fortitude to translate everything, including the obscene poems, into English.

My thanks are due also to Professor Felix Stefanile, who read the entire manuscript and made many helpful suggestions. As usual, my wife has not only provided the sketches which brighten the text but has helped with the manuscript at every stage of the work, from early drafts to proofreading.

Versions of some of the epigrams have been published in the following magazines: Bitterroot, Elizabeth, The Free Lance, The Georgia Review, The Goliards, the goodly co, Kentucky Review, A Nosegay in Black, Poetry Review, Quartet, Scrip, South and West, Southern Poetry Review, Trace, Wormwood Review, and Xenia.

Barriss Mills

West Lafayette, Indiana
August 30, 1967

# THE POETRY OF MARTIAL

Martial is a writer whose virtues and deficiencies seem all on the surface. There is nothing ambiguous about him—nothing tragic or existential. We cannot spin elaborate critical webs about his poems, and they do not invite us to look deeply into the human consciousness or unconscious. He presents himself to us as a quite uncomplicated person and poet, and he does so in a manner more remarkable for its straightforwardness and candor than its literary finesse. There is wit, of course, and there are tricks of language and turns of thought to enhance the wit, but there is none of the elaboration and mystification of style and tone most poets like to set up between themselves and their readers, as though they were special beings with special awarenesses and insights—or at least special ways of seeing things.

If anyone has a "clear, plate-glassy style," it is Martial. And if anyone seems not to have created a mask or persona out of which to write, it is he. Martial seems to talk to us quite simply and directly about himself as he is, without art and without "pose." But we must not let ourselves be deceived. His is an art that conceals art, a pose that seems unposed. And it is a pose based on one of the oldest tricks of social psychology, the trick of never seeming to condescend, of always permitting others to condescend—the trick of the clown or buffoon who makes us laugh *at* him while we are laughing *with* him. Every group has one such, and whatever he loses in dignity and respect is more than made up for in general likability.

Thus Martial presents himself to us as a sycophant, a snob, a sponger—and a thoroughly likable fellow. As we follow him through a day in Rome—attending the levee of a patron, or asserting his right to wear a knight's toga, or wangling a dinner invitation—we are able to feel superior to him. *We* would not toady. *We* would not take such pride in a minor title and the small pension conferred by the emperors. *We* would not stoop to such shifts to get ourselves a free supper. At least, we like to think we would not. And with our condescension goes a feeling that we need not be afraid of liking a fellow who so frankly reveals himself as less dignified than we should like to be.

One of the most striking features of Martial's pose (and it *is* a pose, as clearly defined and consistently maintained as Vergil's epic grandeur and refined antiquarianism, or Lucretius' philosophical astringency, or Catullus' romantic commitment and despair) is the role he assigns to himself as a poet.

In the first place, he chooses to be a minor writer, a composer of "jokes" or "trifles," as he calls them. His patroness is Thalia, the muse of comedy. He renounces epic and tragedy as "windy nonsense" and restricts himself to the epigram, a *genre* which combines wit and brevity with a refusal to deal solemnly with experience.

He sets out to be a popular poet and prides himself on having succeeded. His answer to those who charge him with working on too trifling a scale is that while everyone admires tragedy and epic, it is his jokes and epigrams they buy and read.

He pictures himself as perhaps our first "professional" writer—half genuine poet and half literary hack exploiting his talent to win patronage and popularity. And he illustrates the latter role with a series of outrageously flattering poems addressed to the emperors and a series of purely obscene poems unrelieved by the wit and humor we expect from Martial at his best. Perhaps there is a canny economy of means here—a realization that unction and indecency were sufficient for the purposes of these poems. More likely Martial's wit was simply not engaged in poems written so obviously to win and support his pension, on the one hand, and to titillate the book-buyers, on the other.

He puts himself before us quite openly as a Roman version of the Grub Street scribbler, working at his trade through all moods and weathers, grumbling about its small rewards and the indignities inherent in the patronage system (he even suggests a kind of writers' strike or organized protest when the dole is cut back), and delighting in small triumphs of popularity. He is the minor poet grinding out his verses in a draughty garret three flights up, scrounging for food and clothing and a modicum of self-respect—the prototype of the bourgeois-bohemian artist everywhere and the anti-hero of the sub-world of poetry: the antithesis of Vergil and Horace, basking in a Maecenas' golden favor.

This portrait of the artist as the hard-working practitioner of a precarious craft is not accidental or incidental. It is a deliberate stance, like Trollope's in his *Autobiography*, at once an act of self-revelation and a protest against pomposity in art. Both writers have paid for such iconoclastic honesty in the damage done to their literary reputations, and it probably helped prevent Martial from reaping the big rewards, in patronage and literary stature, in his own day. We admire writers who are noble, like Homer or Longfellow, or romantic, like Catullus or Dylan Thomas. We don't like to be reminded that they are fellows like ourselves whose daily work happens to be putting words together into poems. We prefer that they not be ironic about their own writing, which we like to think of as a mystery or a miracle—a kind of sleight of hand. But Martial, in a gesture of fundamental honesty which compliments our intelligence and rationalizes, if it does not quite excuse, his pandering to emperors and patrons and the public, refuses to play that game with us. Like Trollope, he reveals the ultimate trade secret— that writing is, at least in part, a job like any other.

There is, I think, an ulterior strategy behind Martial's pose as a writer, at least in part, of poems "to order." It is related to the nature of the epigram itself, and of the wit which is its essence.

The epigram, as Martial inherited it from earlier poets, was a rather formless, indeterminate literary *genre*. The word itself means "inscription," and the first epigrams were composed for carving on tombstones or votive tablets, where brevity was the first consideration. Even a quick glance through the many volumes of the Greek Anthology, with their thousands of trivial, uninspired, and repetitious verses, will remind us how *un*witty most of the early epigrams were. Before Martial, epigram meant any brief piece of verse which the anthological zeal of Meleager or Phillipus or Agathias or Cephalus or Planudes happened to preserve, and perhaps only the poet Lucillius consistently anticipated Martial in the intellectual sharpness of his epigrams.

Martial's great accomplishment is to have established wit, rather than mere brevity, as the hallmark of the epigram. Not all his poems are satirical, though they are usually so. He can write movingly of the death of a young girl or a favorite slaveboy. He can write sincere poems praising his friends, and insincere ones praising the emperors. But always, in the epigrams that work, there are turns of thought or phrase which we may call wit in the largest sense.

Wit may be defined as the application of intellect to human experience to point up the incongruity, and often the absurdity, of much of it. Wit sets the things we do or say or think or feel over against the things a purely rational being might do or say or think or feel. Its targets are most frequently the inconsistencies and disproportions in our attitudes toward ourselves and others and the ways these manifest themselves in our behavior—especially our egotism and vanity and the self-deceptions these involve us in.

Each of us is in one sense the center of the universe and a culmination of history: we cannot help feeling this is so, from moment to moment as we make our way through life. All our values are based, in part, on the supreme importance, to ourselves, *of* ourselves. But seen objectively, most of us seem the merest digits in the sum total of things. And even from the point of view of a neighbor or a friend, our self-importance suffers a considerable diminution.

Wit fixes on this disparity of values as a source of mockery and fun. How large we loom in our own thoughts! Yet how easily others seem to forget that we even exist! No wonder we strive so desperately to prove to others and ourselves that we *cannot* be ignored—by trying to attain social status or political power; by amassing wealth and surrounding ourselves with servants and imposing houses; by insisting that we be loved, within the family group or in marriage or in promiscuous affairs; by writing poems for others to read.

Martial is a master of this ironic view of human experience, and it pervades the epigram as he developed it and as it has persisted ever since. Yet wit and irony are products of a highly intellectual point of view, and there is a kind of paradox in the fact that such a cerebral poet as Martial should have been truly popular—should have had the whole Roman world, as Martial boasts, laughing at his poems. The truly popular writer is more likely to be one who somehow puffs up our egos, or flatters our vanities, or glosses over our foolishnesses. The best-seller usually tells us, in one way or another, that we are as good or as wise or as important as we'd like to think we are, and that we can, if only vicariously, be loved or feared or respected. Martial tells us none of these things.

On the other hand, we all like jokes, even black and bitter ones sometimes, to remind us of our failings and our frailty and to restore the balance, now and then, between the dignity in which we clothe ourselves and the pettiness of much that we are. Like Shakespeare's kings and dukes with their court fools and jesters, we need our public "wits" to save us from excesses of self-deception and pride.

Martial was no court fool. The emperors, having permitted themselves to be deified in life, seem not to have shared the old Greek fear that *hubris* might bring divine retribution, and Martial hardly dares risk a joke in addressing these exalted personages. But he does seem to have thought of himself as a kind of *public* jester, reminding his Roman readers who had *not* been deified of their common humanity and the humility that ought to accompany it. This seems to be the real function of his satire, rather than the traditionally accepted one of reforming society by exposing its follies and abuses. Perhaps this is the real function of all satire and irony, all wit and jokes—to keep us humanly humble.

But wit and irony and satire have a harsher side. As Freud has observed, a joke may be a veiled attack on the person we tell it to, and wit is often a venting of our aggressions, consciously or unconsciously. It has elements of cruelty and sadism. In the public mind most irony is equated with sarcasm, with its implications of ill will, and we sense a tendency to twist the knife in the wound even in Lear's famous fool.

There is something cold, detached, even condescending about most wit and irony. They seem too cerebral to be fully humane. Saints and lovers do not use them.

It seems clear that Martial recognized these dangers inherent in the epigram and took steps to avoid them, whether deliberately or through the natural tact of the public entertainer. There is sympathy, on the whole, for the objects of his satire. Their vanity and folly are usually shown as a kind of bumbling and transparent self-deception rather than as anything vicious or harmful to others. He seems to say that vanity and folly are the natural products of our humanity and we are no less likable for them.

Further, Martial's satire is directed as often against himself as against others. He is at least as quick to make fun of his own stupidities as anyone else's, and his own involvement enables us to accept his criticism of ourselves with better grace. It helps save his irony from coldness and turns his wit into humor.

Finally, as I have suggested above, Martial has humanized his own role as satirist and ironist by assuming the stance of a hard-working professional rather than a gentleman writer. He invites us to laugh at him and look down on him, even while he is making fun of us all. Like Shakespeare's fools, he is "privileged"—he can speak as freely and saucily as he chooses because we need not take anything he says, as a public jester and professional buffoon, very seriously.

Most followers of Martial in other respects have failed to imitate his tact in these matters. They have seemed to rail at us, like angry parents or schoolmarms. Perhaps they have felt that they would reform society, or us, and "correct" our follies and vanities that way. But like naughty children we resist the admonitions of our betters—or we close our ears. They have failed to earn, as Martial has done by publicly humbling himself, the license for public criticism.

From his position of weakness (which is strength) Martial makes fun of almost every aspect of Roman life in the first century after Christ: its dinners and drinking parties, its public baths and public spectacles, its lawsuits, its noisy, crowded streets—and its preoccupation with social status and money and dress, its cynicism (and his) about marriage and sex and even friendship, its reverence for wealth and influence, its social climbers and *nouveaux riches,* its struggling poets and arrogant patrons.

And he is an equally mocking observer of his own behavior, as a working poet fully conscious of the necessity of pleasing his readers and his patrons, and of not offending the emperors and the court which had granted him a knighthood and small pension. He shows himself jealous and wittily abusive of rival poets, wary of plagiarists, and always at war with the critics, like most poets before and since. He calculates the ups and downs of the dole like a small businessman studying the market reports. And he publishes (and advertizes) his books of poems as frequently as he thinks the traffic will bear.

We find in Martial the eternal types of pettiness and pretense in which we all share—or in which Martial, at least, is quite willing to admit he shares: self-esteem, envy, pose, extravagance and stinginess, pomposity, gluttony, drunkenness, an eye for the main chance, an infinite capacity for flattering others when it may get us something we want and for rising above such tactics when they will not—all presented, good-naturedly and without surprise, as part of the human condition. The eternal sources of humor and the oldest jokes are here, as well as fresher materials: marrying for money, flirting with other men's wives, the girls who play hard to get and the girls who just want to play, the absent-minded professor, the doctor who kills off his patients, the patron who is never at home to his proteges because he's off dancing attendance on *his* patron, the friends who expect free copies of an author's books and the author who wonders if his circulation is made up entirely of such free copies. All this is presented as perfectly natural, considering what we are, and decidedly funny, considering what we'd like to think we are.

So pervasive is Martial's irony (directed, as often as not, against himself) that he strikes us at first as very nearly the complete cynic—the citizen of a corrupt and dissolute society partaking fully of that corruption, though fully aware of his participation in it. We do not find in him any strong sense of moral or social indignation—any considered belief in religion, or in patriotism, or in love and marriage (sex seems to be, for him, a commodity one obtains as cheaply as possible, like food and clothing), or friendship. For Catullus, love and friendship, at least, were necessary beliefs, however often the realities of experience might betray them. Martial seems never to have married, never to have been really in love, and not to have been dependent upon close friendship.

Martial offers no social, political, or economic remedies for the ills of Roman society which he satirizes. He is as unpolitical as his "master" Catullus. Economically, he seems to be concerned only with doing the best he can for himself in a situation where money is power and a mere poet is in a weak bargaining position. And his only reaction to the social order, or disorder, of Rome is a snobbish complacency in his own knighthood—conferred, we may suppose, for flatteries received. He does yearn, occasionally, for escape from the system and the city itself—temporarily, to his tiny Nomentan farm or his cousin Julius Martial's country house, or, more permanently, back to Bilbilis, the small town in Spain from which he had come as a young man and to which he returned to live out the last few years of his life. But he finds the simpler, quieter ways of provincial life a mixed blessing after thirty-four years in the capital and is frankly homesick, in retirement, for Rome.

Yet cynic is not the word for so good-natured a satirist, and one so willing to play the game himself, however absurd its rules and its goals may show themselves, at times, to be. I should call him, rather, a realist—one who accepts things as they are and does not feel any very strong hope, or even desire, that they will change. If Rome is not the best of all possible worlds, neither is Bilbilis, and perhaps, man being what he is, they are as good as he deserves. At any rate, Martial seems to have felt about Rome as Dr. Johnson felt about London: it was good enough for *him*.

For Martial likes Rome, and the extravagance of its shows and its pleasures, even when he is satirizing them. He never gets over the country boy's delight in the variety and excitement of the metropolis. Bilbilis may be a more wholesome place to be born in and to die in, but Rome is the center, where money and power are, however little Martial may have shared in them, and where literature is. It is Rome, at the height of her recklessness and glory, before Christianity or the Germanic tribes or overextended frontiers or corrupt generals and emperors brought her down, that Martial gives us—day by day and year by year as he lived in it and wrote in it, clear-eyed and without illusions but delightfully involved in it all—better than any other poet.

There is more to Martial than a sharp wit and skill as a teller of funny and often bawdy jokes, even if he seems to claim no more than that for himself. There is Rome, in all moods and at all hours of the day, and the people in it, presented satirically but also realistically and with sympathy. And there is an honesty—a complacency, even—about human pretensions and folly that goes beyond wit to humor. Like Rabelais and Cervantes and Shakespeare and Dickens and Mark Twain, Martial tells us something very true, and sometimes rather touching, about ourselves that we need to remember and too often prefer to forget. Though he works on a smaller scale than any of them, Martial shares the great humorists' wonder and delight in man's outrageous foolishness.

# Preface to Book I

I trust I've shown such restraint in my little books that no one with a clear conscience can object to them. They have their fun without sacrificing respect for even the least important persons—something the older epigrammatists cared so little about that they blackened the names of real people, and even of great ones.

My fame as a poet can be established at less cost, I hope. And a reputation for mere cleverness is the last thing I'm after. But malicious critics must refrain from tampering with the straightforward meaning of my jokes, and rewriting my epigrams. It's hardly proper to demonstrate one's own ingenuity on another man's book.

I'd apologize for the honest bawdiness of my language (the language, that is, of the epigram) if it were original with me. Catullus wrote this way, and so did Marsus, and Pedo, and Gaetulicus, and everyone else we still read with interest. But if there's anyone so ostentatiously puritanical that he thinks it's wrong ever to speak plain Latin, he can stop reading with this preface, or better yet with the title page.

Epigrams are written for people who enjoy watching the naked dances in honor of the goddess Flora. Let no Cato enter my theater, or if he does, let him watch like everybody else. I suppose I'm within my rights in closing this preface with some verses:

> You knew what wanton Flora
> finds pleasing at her festival:
> naughty jokes, honest vulgarity.
> Then why, sober-sided Cato,
> did you come to the theater?
> Did you put in an appearance
> in order to stalk out again?

## I, i

Hic est quem legis ille, quem requiris,
toto notus in orbe Martialis
argutis epigrammaton libellis:
cui, lector studiose, quod dedisti
viventi decus atque sentienti
rari post cineres habent poetae.

# BOOK I

## I, i

Here he is—the one you read,
the one you ask for—Martial,
recognized the world over
for his witty books of epigrams.
Learned reader, you've given him
(while he's still alive to enjoy it)
the glory poets rarely get
after they've turned to ashes.

## I, ii

Whoever wants my poems
beside him wherever he goes
to turn to for companionship
on the longest journey, buy these,
got up in a pocket edition
wrapped in parchment. The great poets
come in bound volumes, boxed.
You can carry me in one hand.
But in case you're uncertain where
I'm for sale and are wandering
aimlessly all over town,
I'll direct you where you'll be sure
to find me : hunt up Secundus,
learned Lucensis' freedman
behind the gates to the Temple
of Peace and Minerva's Forum.

## I, iv

If you happen to run across
my books, Caesar, lay aside
that stern glance that rules the world.
Your triumphs will have taught you
to put up with jokes, and a leader
can subject himself to witticisms
without shame. Please read my poems
the same way you'd watch Thymele
or Latinus the mimic. A censor
can wink at innocent fun.
My little books may be naughty,
but my life is clean.

## I, x

Gemellus wants Maronilla
to marry him. He argues,
pleads, sends presents. He
can hardly wait.
                    Is she
so beautiful?
                    On the contrary,
there's no one more hideous.
Then what does he see in her
to attract him?
                    She coughs.

## I, xvii

Titus urges me to plead cases
and says "There's money in it."
There's money in farming, too,
Titus—if you're a farmer.

## I, xx

Tell me, Caecilianus,
are you crazy? With this mob
you've invited looking on,
you're gobbling up all the mushrooms
yourself. What can I pray for
worthy of such a gullet
and belly? Eat such mushrooms
as Emperor Claudius ate.

## I, xxvii

Last night I invited you
(I guess it was after I'd finished
off a dozen drinks, Procillus)
to have dinner with me today.
You considered the matter settled
then and there, and took careful note
of my drunken words—a habit
that could lead to all kinds of trouble!
I hate a drinking-companion
with a memory, Procillus.

## I, xxviii

If you think it's yesterday's wine
Acerra stinks of, you're wrong.
He never stops drinking till daylight.

## I, xxx

Diaulus used to be a surgeon.
Now he's an undertaker.
He's still laying them out
with his best bedside manner.

## I, xxxii

I don't like you, Sabidius.
Don't ask me why. I only know
I just can't stand you.

## I, xxxv

You take me to task for writing
poems that aren't as prissy
and prim as they might be, Cornelius.
Not the kind a schoolmaster
would read aloud in the classroom.
But my little books wouldn't satisfy
(anymore than husbands can
their wives) without a little sex.

Would you want me to write a wedding-song
without using the words that wedding-songs
always use? Would you cover up
Flora's nymphs with a lot of clothing
or let prostitutes hide their shamefulness
under ladies' robes? There's a rule
that merry songs can't be merry
unless they're a bit indecent.

So forget your prudishness, please,
and spare my jokes and my naughtiness,
and don't try to castrate my poems.
Nothing's worse than Priapus posing
as a eunuch of Cybele.

### I, xxxvi

If you, Lucanus, or you,
Tullus, either one, were confronted
with the fate of Leda's Spartan sons,
there'd be noble rivalry
of fraternal love between you—
each choosing to give up his life
for his brother.  And whoever
went down first to shadowy hell
would say "Live your life out, brother,
and live mine for me too."

### I, xxxvii

You empty your bowels, Bassus,
in a gold pot, without shame.
Poor pot!  But when you drink,
it's from ordinary glass.
You spend more money on your shitting.

### I, xxxviii

Those poems you're always reciting
are mine, Fidentinus.
But your terrible recitations
are beginning to make them yours.

## I, xliii

There we were, twice thirty of us—
your invited guests last night,
Mancinus—and nothing on the table
except one boar.  No grapes,
vine-ripened.  No apples, sweet
as honeycomb.  No pears
dangling from long, thin straws.
No pomegranates, with their colors
like short-lived roses.


No cheesebaskets, delivered
from the country near Sassina.
No Picenian olive-jars.
Only that boar, and a small one
at that—so tiny a pygmy
could have strangled it with his bare hands.
And not a thing for dessert.


All we could do was look on.
Even the Arena serves up
that kind of boar.  I hope,
after such a trick, you'll never
be served another boar, but serve
yourself, instead, like Charidemus,
as a dinner for a boar.

## I, lv

Fronto, distinguished in learning
and war—do you want to know
in a word what your friend Marcus
really wants? It's this: to be
tiller of his own little farm.
He delights in country laziness,
however poor. Why should anyone
spend his time in elegant houses
of cold marble, bringing with him
his morning greetings, like a fool,
if, blessed with the rich bounty
of woods and fields, he can open
his nets full of game by the fire,
or pull out the wriggling fish
on a trembling line, or pour
golden honey from a red jar?
For whom the bailiff's fat wife
spreads a rickety table and cooks
his own eggs over homemade charcoal.
If anyone doesn't love me,
let him shun this kind of life
and live palefaced by choice
in the ceremonious town.

## I, lvii

What kind of girl do I
like best or least? Flaccus,
I can't stand pushovers
or the ones who make the game
too difficult. I prefer
the intermediate kind,
somewhere between those two.
But save me from girls that drive you
crazy or bore you to death.

## I, lxi

Verona loves the meters
of her learned poet, Catullus.
Mantua's happy with her Vergil.
Padua's famous for her Livy
and Stella and Flaccus as well.
The water-bearing Nile is proud
of Apollodorus, and Ovid
is honored by the Pelignians.
Eloquent Cordova brags
of two Senecas and the one-
and-only Lucan. Merry
Cadiz delights in her Canius,
Emerita in Decianus,
my friend. And our Bilbilis
will be proud of you someday,
Lucinianus, and mention
me too, perhaps, in passing.

## I, lxiii

You ask me to read my epigrams
aloud to you. Nothing doing!
You don't care about hearing them,
Celer. You want to steal them.

## I, lxx

Off you go, little book, to Proculus'
magnificent house. Say "good morning"
in your most respectful manner.

How do you get there? I'll tell you.
Start out past Castor's temple
and ancient Vesta's virgin house.
Look next for that holy hill,
the Palatine. It's gleaming
with statues of our great leader.

Don't let your admiration
for the shining Colossus detain you,
though it's bigger than the one at Rhodes.
Turn there where you see the roof
of drunken Lyaeus' house—
where Cybele's rotunda
stands painted with Corybants.

Right in front of you on the left
a house with a bright facade
and lofty portico invites you
inside. Head for this and don't worry
about being snubbed or sneered at
at the door. The gates are always open
wide. And there never was a house
more dear to Apollo and the Muses.

But if he asks "Why didn't
Martial come himself, all the same?"
you can tell him "No one could write
these poems, whatever they're worth,
if he spent his time paying calls."

## I, lxxi

We'll drink six drinks to Laevia
and seven for Justina.
Five for Lycas, four for Lyde,
and for Ida, three.  We'll drink
a drink for each letter in the names
of all the loving ladies
in bumpers of Falernian.
Then if none of them show up here
Sleep will come to me instead.

## I, lxxiii

There wasn't a man in the city
who'd touch your wife for free,
Caecilianus, when your doors
stood open.  Now that you've posted
guards, a whole crowd of lechers
are standing in line.  You really
are an ingenious fellow.

## I, lxxv

If you decide to give Linus
only half of what he asks for
rather than trust him with all of it,
you'll only lose half as much.

## I, lxxvii

Charinus is in perfect health
and still he's pale.
Charinus drinks sparingly
and still he's pale.
Charinus has a cast-iron stomach
and still he's pale.
Charinus takes sun-baths
and still he's pale.
Charinus puts rouge on his cheeks
and still he's pale.
Charinus indulges himself
in every kind of debauchery
and he still can't blush.


## I, lxxxvi

Novius lives next door to me.
We could shake hands through my windows.
Everyone envies me and thinks
I must be happy all day long
with such a neighbor close by.

Yet he's really as far removed from me
as Terentianus, who's governor
of Syene, in Egypt, these days.
I can never have dinner with him
or even see him and talk with him,
and there's no one in the whole city
so near and yet so far away.

Either I must move farther off
or he must.  Just live next door
to Novius, or even share
the same house with him, if you never
want to see Novius at all.

## I, lxxxvii

So as not to smell too strongly
of yesterday's wine, Fescennia,
you've gobbled down far too many
of Cosmus's lozenges.
This stains your teeth but doesn't
cover anything up when a belch
bubbles up from your lower regions.
Has it ever occurred to you
that the stink may be even stronger,
mixed with drugs, and carry farther,
doubled in strength? Give up
these obvious tricks and transparent
subterfuges and let yourself
be just plain drunk.

## I, lxxxviii

Alcimus, stolen from your master
in your growing years—Lavican
earth is covering you now
with its delicate turf. Receive
from me no tottering pile
of marble which wasted labor
bequeaths to ruin and dust,
but graceful boxwood instead
and the orchard trees' deep shade
and green grass wet with my tears.
Take these, boy that I loved,
as the monuments of my sorrow.
Here your name will live forever.
And when Lachesis has spun
my own last years to the end,
I charge that my ashes be buried
in no other way than this.

## I, lxxxix

Cinna, you're always chattering
in everybody's ear.
Even the things it's permissible
to gossip about in a roomful
of listeners. You laugh
in the ear, complain, accuse,
vent your grievances. You sing
in the ear, express opinions,
keep silent, shout. This sickness
of yours has taken such a hold
on you, Cinna, you even speak
your praise of Caesar in the ear.

## I, xci

You criticize my poems,
Laelius, but you never
publish your own. Either
stop pulling mine to pieces
or let us have a look at yours.

## I, xcv

We know why you're always shouting
and interrupting the debates,
Aelius. You're not doing it
for the fun of it. You're hoping
to be paid to hold your tongue.

I, xcvii

When everybody's shouting,
and only then, you speak,
Naevolus, and consider yourself
a pleader and an orator.
On this principle there's no one
who can't be eloquent.
Listen! Everyone's silent:
Say something, Naevolus.

I, xcviii

Diodorus is bringing suit
in the courts, Flaccus. He also
suffers from a gouty foot.
But he doesn't intend to pay
his lawyer anything.
The gout has reached his hands.

## I, xcix

A little while ago, Calenus,
you didn't have a full two million,
but you were so open-handed
and generous and entertained
so lavishly that your friends
all wished you had ten.  Some god
overheard our prayers and pleadings
and in seven months, I think it was,
four deaths had brought you what we asked for.

But just as if nothing at all
had been left you—as if, instead,
you'd been robbed of your two million—-
you've turned into such a miser,
such a starving fellow, that the one
decent banquet you give all year
you put on at the trifling expense
of a few dirty coppers, and we,
your seven old eating-companions,
cost you about half a pound
of counterfeit coin.  What rewards
shall we pray for, for such kindness?

We'll wish you a hundred million,
Calenus.  If you get it,
you'll starve yourself to death.

## I, cii

If you ask me, Lycoris,
that fellow who did your painting
of Venus was currying favor
with her enemy, Minerva.

## I, ciii

You used to say, Scaevola,
when you still weren't rich enough—
quite—to be called a gentleman:
"If only the mighty gods
would make me a millionaire,
how I'd live it up—lavishly
and open-handedly." The gods
laughed in their easy-going way
and gave you what you asked for.

Since then your toga is dirtier
by far, and your cloak shabbier,
and your shoe-soles have been mended
three or four times. If you've got
ten olives for the dinner table
you hold back more than half of them
and every meal provides left-overs
for another one. You drink
cheap red Veientan wine
down to the dregs. And the chick-peas
you serve lukewarm cost a penny,
and so does your lady-love.

I ought to take you to court
for being a cheat and a swindler!
Live a little, Scaevola, or give
that million back to the gods.

### I, cvi

You're always adding water
to your wine, Rufus. And you sip
the diluted stuff, now and then,
but only when a friend insists.

Has Naevia promised you a night
of fun, and you're staying sober
to be better in bed? But you sigh,
and say nothing, and sigh again.

So she must have said no. Then drink
all you want. Drown your troubles in wine.
What's stopping you, Rufus? There's nothing
to look forward to but sleep.

### I, cvii

My dear friend Lucius Julius,
you're always preaching at me
"Write something big. You're a lazy
fellow." Well, give me the leisure
Maecenas used to give his Horace
and his Vergil and I'd write
poems to outlive the centuries
and snatch my name from oblivion.
Even oxen won't bear the yoke
in sterile fields willingly.
A rich soil can be tiring
but the work itself is fun.

## I, cviii

You've a lovely house. I hope
it stands and flourishes for years.
But it's over beyond the Tiber,
while my attic room looks out
on Vipsanius' laurel gardens.
I'm already growing old
in this place. It's a long way to go
to greet you in the mornings, Gallus,
at your house. It would be worth it,
even if you lived further off.

But it can't matter much to you
whether I'm one more caller
in a toga, and it means a lot
to me, Gallus, not to be one.
I'll greet you myself at dinnertime.
My book says "Good morning" for me.


## I, cix

Issa's naughtier
than Catullus' sparrow.
Issa's purer
than the kiss of a dove.
Issa's more flirtatious
than any girl.
Issa's more precious
than the jewels of India.
Issa's Publius' pet lapdog.

When she whimpers, you'd imagine
she's speaking. She's sensitive
to her master's moods of sadness
and joy. She cuddles up
against his neck and sleeps

so quietly that her breathing
can't be heard.

When nature's demands
overcome her, she never spoils
the bedspread with a single drop.
She wakes you with a gentle paw
and warns you to put her down
from the bed. And when she's finished
she begs to be lifted again.
So great is the modesty
of this chaste little dog that love
is unknown to her. We can't find
a suitable mate for so delicate
a lady.

And so that death
won't steal her away from him
altogether, Publius had
her picture painted. You'll see there
an Issa so lifelike that Issa
herself doesn't look more like herself.
In short, if you put Issa
beside her picture, you can't tell
which one's real and which one's painted.

## I, cx

You complain that my epigrams
are too long, Velox. But you
yourself write nothing at all.
You take the brevity prize.

## I, cxiii

All the foolish things I wrote
as a boy or young man, years ago—
all the nonsense I myself
have forgotten ever writing—
you can get from Pollius Quintus
Valerianus, the bookseller,
if you feel like wasting your time,
reader, and spending good hours
badly. It's because of him
my trifles aren't allowed to die.


## I, cxvii

Whenever we meet, Lupercus,
you immediately ask
"May I send a boy to pick up
your little book of epigrams?
I'll be getting it back to you
as soon as I've read it."

        You needn't
put your boy to all that trouble,
Lupercus. It's a long way,
if he starts out from the Pear Tree,
and I live up three flights of stairs—
long ones at that. You can find
what you're asking for closer by.

You go past the Agriletum
every day, I suppose. Just across
from Caesar's forum is a shop
with handbills plastered all over
the doorway. In less than a minute
you can read all the poets' names.

You'll find me there. And you won't
even have to ask Atrectum
(that's the bookseller's name). He'll hand you,
out of the first pigeon-hole
or the second, for five denarii,
a Martial polished with pumice-stone
and decorated with purple.

"You're not worth that much," you say?
Maybe you're right, Lupercus.

# BOOK II

## II, i

You might have contained three hundred
epigrams, easily, my book.
But who'd have put up with you then,
or read you through? As it is
you'll learn the advantages
of being short. First of all,
I waste less paper. Next,
my copyist can get through you
in an hour and needn't spend
so much of his time on my trifles.
And third, if you're read aloud
to someone, no matter how bad
you are, you won't be boring.
A guest can finish you before
his toddy has a chance to cool.
Are you thinking such brevity
will save you? Alas, for many
you'll still seem much too long.

## II, v

Decianus, as I hope to thrive,
I'd like to be with you day and night.
But it's two miles from my place to yours,
and when I have to come back,
that's four. And often you're not
at home. Or if you are,
they often tell me you're not.
Or often you haven't time
for anyone but your clients
or yourself. Still, I wouldn't mind
going the two miles to see you.
What I object to is going
four and not seeing you at all.

## II, vi

So much for your encouraging me
to publish my poems, Severus.
You read a mere two pages and skip
to the last one and let out
enormous yawns. And yet these
are the poems you used to ask me
to recite again, and you'd copy
them down on your best writing-tablets
immediately. And these
are the poems you used to carry,
every one, to all sorts of parties
and the theater, in your pocket.
These are the ones, or better ones
you've not seen before. What's the use
of my making a book so thin
it's no fatter than the stick it's rolled on,

if it takes you three full days
to read it? Never were verses
so lazily enjoyed before.
What a weary traveller you are
to give up so soon! If you had
to make a journey to Bovillae
would you break the trip at Camenae?
So much for your encouraging me
to publish my poems!

## II, vii

Atticus, you speak charmingly,
plead cases charmingly,
write charming stories and verses.
You're a charming grammarian
and astrologer, and you sing
and dance charmingly, Atticus, charmingly.
You play the harp charmingly
and charmingly toss the ball.
Since you do nothing really well,
but everything charmingly,
what shall I call you, Atticus?
A magnificent busybody.

## II, viii

Reader, if any of these pieces
strike you as too obscure
or not quite good enough Latin,
don't blame me. The copyist spoiled them
in hurrying to get my verses
ready for you. If you still think
it's my fault rather than his,
then I think you lack judgment.
"But some of them are bad!"
you say. As if I'd deny
what's obvious. They're bad,
but you don't make better ones.


## II, xi

Look, Rufus, how Selius' face
is clouded over. How he paces
the portico after the others
have gone. How his gloomy expression
speaks without words of something
unpleasant. How his ugly nose
almost touches the ground. How he beats
his breast and pulls at his hair.

And yet he's not mourning the death
of a brother or a friend.
Every one of his sons is alive—
and I hope they go on living.
His wife and his goods and his slaves
are safe. And he hasn't been cheated
by his tenants or his overseers.

What's his trouble, then? Nobody's
invited him out to dinner.

## II, xiii

The judge is demanding his fee.
And so is your lawyer, Sextus.
My advice is, pay your creditor.

## II, xviii

I wangle your dinner invitation,
Maximus. It's embarrassing,
but I do it. And you wangle
someone else's. So we're even.

I come to pay a morning call,
and they tell me you've already
gone to pay another. So we're even.

I swell the rout around you
in your progress through the city.
You swell another's. So we're even.

It's bad enough to be a flunky.
I don't want to be a flunky's flunky.
A patron, Maximus, shouldn't
need a patron of his own.

## II, xxv

You're always promising, Galla,
but never give me what I ask for.
Since you always go back on your word,
Galla, say "no" next time.

## II, xxvii

Whenever Selius is angling
for a dinner, he's a great applauder—
whether you're reciting poems
or pleading a case: "That's great!
Tremendous! Witty! That settles him!
Bravo! Lovely!" That will do.
You've earned your dinner. Shut up.

## II, xxix

Rufus, see that fellow lounging
on the front benches, whose hand
even at this distance is shining
with sardonyx, and whose cloak
has drunk the Tyrian purple
more than once, and whose toga
is whiter than untouched snow.

Whose well-oiled hair perfumes
the whole theater of Marcellus,
and whose depilated arms
shine so smoothly. A senator's boots,
bright red, brand new, the best leather,
decorated with crescent moons,
adorn his uncalloused feet.

And his forehead's plastered all over
with beauty-patches like stars.
Why the patches? Peel them off
and look at the brands underneath.

## II, xxx

As it happened, I asked for a loan
of twenty thousand sesterces—
not too great a sacrifice
even as a gift. What's more,
I asked it of an old friend,
well-heeled, whose moneyboxes
are stuffed to overflowing.
He told me "You could get rich
pleading cases."

       Give me the thing
I asked for, Gaius. I didn't
ask you for advice.

## II, xxxvi

I don't say you should curl your hair,
but you could comb it.
I don't say your body should be oiled,
but you could take a bath.
You needn't have a eunuch's beard
or a jailbird's. I don't insist
upon too much manliness,
Pannychus, or too little.
As it is, your legs are hairy
and your chest is shaggy with bristles,
but your mind, Pannychus, is bald.

## II, xxxvii

Reaching here and there, you sweep up
whatever's on the table: sow's tits,
pork ribs, a woodcock meant for two,
half a mullet, a whole pike,
a filet of eel and a chicken leg,
and a pigeon dripping with white sauce.
And when you've stuffed all these dainties
in a sodden napkin, you give them
to your boy to carry home.

Meanwhile the rest of us recline
at the table with nothing to do.
If you've any shame, give us back
our dinner. I didn't invite you
for breakfast, Caecilianus.

## II, xxxviii

You ask me, Linus, what good
my farm at Nomentum does me?
It does one thing for me, Linus:
I can get away from you there.

## II, xli

I think it was Ovid who said
"Laugh, if you're wise, girl, laugh."
But he didn't mean it for all girls.
Or even if he meant it for all girls,
he didn't mean it for you.

You're not a girl, Maximia,
and you have three teeth, the color
of pitch or boxwood.  And therefore,
if you've any faith in your mirror
or in me, you ought to be afraid
of laughing, the same way Spanius
is afraid of a breeze that might ruffle
his hair, or Priscus of someone's
dirty fingers on his cloak,
or powdered Fabella of a rainstorm,
or painted Sabella of daylight.

You ought to put on an expression
more woeful than Hecuba's
or Andromache's.  Stay away
from Philistius' rowdy farces
and other such lively entertainments
or any witty impertinences
that relax the lips in outright laughter.

You should sit by some grieving mother
or someone who's mourning a husband
or beloved brother, and indulge yourself
only with the tragic muse.

Take my advice and weep,
if you are wise, girl, weep.

## II, xliii

"Share and share alike between friends,"
you say.  But is this the sharing
you preach about night and day
with such eloquence, Candidus?

You're wrapped in a Tarentine toga
washed in the Galaesus River,
or one made of wool which Parma
supplies from its choicest flocks.
As for mine, you'd think it had suffered
at the horns of an angry bull,
and even the first straw dummy
they throw out into the arena
would refuse to claim it for its own.

The land of Cadmus sends you
purple shawls.  My scarlet one
wouldn't sell for three sesterces.
Your circular table-tops—
cross-sections of Libyan citruswood—
rest on legs of Indian ivory.
My beechwood table is propped
on a brick.  Enormous mullets
fill up your gold-chased dishes.
A red crawfish lies in the middle
of my red earthenware plate.
Servants wait on you in troops
like Olympian cupbearers.
My hand is Ganymede to me.

From among such riches, Candidus,
can you offer your old friend nothing
and still say "share alike"?

## II, xliv

If I buy a slave, or a toga
of brushed wool, or three or four pounds,
let's say, of plated silver—
Sextus the money-lender,
an old friend who lives nearby,
starts worrying that I'll ask him
for a loan.  He mutters to himself,
loud enough so I can hear:
"Let's see.  I owe Secundus
seven thousand, and Phoebus four,
and Philetus eleven, and I haven't
two cents in my moneybox."
That's a fine way to treat an old friend!
It's bad enough saying no
when you're asked, Sextus.  It's worse
saying no before anyone asks you.

## II, xlvi

Like Hybla's many-colored flowers
when Sicilian bees are ravishing
the short-lived spring, your clothes-presses
shine with cloaks, one piled on another,
and your closets are bright with dinner-robes
beyond counting, and a whole tribe
could be dressed in your white togas
to which more than one Apulian
flock has contributed.
Yet you look with indifference
on your half-starved, shivering friend
and escort, ragged and cold.
It's sinful!  What would it cost you
(poor man, what are you afraid of?)
to cheat—not yourself, Naevolus,
but the moths—of a couple of rags?

## II, xlviii

Decent wine, decent meat,
a barber, a place to take a bath,
a chessboard and a few books
(provided I can choose them).
One friend who's not too dull,
a tall, unbearded serving-boy
and a girl for my boy to love.
Give me these, even at a place
like Butunti, and you can have
Nero's warm baths, Rufus.

## II, lii

Dasius has his own way
of charging the people who come
to his bathing-place. He told
big-breasted Spatale
she must pay for three, and she paid.

## II, liii

Do you really want to be free?
No you don't, Maximus. You're lying.
But if you do, here's the way
to go about it. You'll be free
if you turn down all invitations
to dinner, and drink cheap wine,
and laugh at poor Cinna's gold-
encrusted dishes. And content yourself
with a toga like mine and two-bit
whores and an attic-room
you have to stoop to walk into.
If you've got that kind of courage
and strength of mind, you'll be able
to live your life more freely
than any Parthian king.

## II, lvi

Your wife has a bad reputation
among the Libyan tribes,
Gallus. They accuse her—
unjustly—of immoderate greed.
They're simply lying. She isn't
in the habit of accepting favors.
Not at all. She gives them—to everyone.


## II, lvii

That fellow you see promenading
in an amethyst gown, so leisurely,
as he makes his progress through the crowd—
whom even my old friend Publius
can't outshine in cloaks, or Cordus,
who's A-1 in cloakwearing—
who's followed by a mob of spongers
in togas, and long-haired slaves
carrying his sedan-chair
fitted out with new straps and curtains—
that fellow, this very minute,
pawned his ring at Cladus' pawnshop
for a measly eight sesterces
to buy himself dinner with.


## II, lix

I'm called The Tidbit. You can see
what I am—a tiny banquet-room.
But look, there's an excellent view
of Caesar's tomb from here.
So rumple the couches. Call
for wine and roses. And bathe
yourself in perfume. The god—
Augustus himself—admonishes you
to remember your own death.

## II, lx

Hyllus, my boy, while you're sleeping
with the captain's wife, you're afraid
of getting the kind of punishment
a boy deserves. But look out!
In the midst of your fun, he'll geld you.
"But that's not legal," you tell me.
So what? The thing you're doing—
do you call that legal, Hyllus?

## II, lxiii

You never had more than a hundred
thousand sesterces, Milichus,
and they went to purchase Leda
in the Via Sacra. Too much
to spend on love, Milichus,
even if you were rich.
"But I'm not in love," you reply.
Then it's even more extravagant!

## II, lxviii

Don't think me insolent, Olus,
for calling you by your name
nowadays instead of "Patron"
or "Master" as I used to do.
I've bought my freedman's cap
with everything I possessed.

A man needs patrons and masters
if he isn't master of himself
and covets the same things patrons
and masters covet. But once
he can get along without a slave,
he can get along without a master.

## II, lxxi

No one's more candid than you are,
Caecilianus. I've noticed
whenever I read a few couplets
you immediately quote lines
from Catullus or Marsus. Perhaps
that's meant as a compliment—
to make my verses sound better
by reading some not quite so good.
I'd like to believe it. All the same,
I'd feel better if you recited
your own poems, Caecilianus.

## II, lxxvii

As a critic, Cosconius,
you'd make a good wheel-greaser.
You call my epigrams too long.
But that's like saying the Colossus
is too tall, or that boy-figurine
Brutus loved so much is too short.
You ought to know, if you don't,
that often two pages of Marsus
or learned Pedo are devoted
to a single idea. Nothing's
too long if you can't leave anything
out. But you, Cosconius,
write couplets that are too long.

## II, lxxx

Running away from an enemy,
Fannius killed himself.
I ask you, isn't that crazy—
dying, so as not to die?

## II, lxxxii

Why punish your slave, Ponticus,
by cutting out his tongue?
Don't you know people will talk,
even if he can't?

## II, lxxxv

A bottle of boiled water, iced,
and wrapped in light wickerwork—
that will be my Saturnalia
present for you.  If you complain
because I'm sending a summer gift
in December, you can retaliate
by sending me a light-weight toga.

## II, lxxxvi

Just because I don't pride myself
on writing poems that read backward
as well as forward, or ones
with a secret, filthy meaning
when read the wrong way round,
or the kind where a word's repeated
like an echo in the Greekish manner,
or soft, unmanly galliambics
such as eloquent Attis might utter—
that doesn't mean I'm incompetent
as a poet, Classicus,

though you seem to think it does.
Would you order Ladas, the race-horse,
to trot along the narrow path
of an acrobat's plank? It's degrading
to take too much trouble with trifles,
and hard work spent on foolishness
is stupid. Let Palaemon
write poems to please his circle
of flatterers. I'd rather
reach the ears of a chosen few.


## II, xc

Quintillian, great moderator
of youth's impetuosity,
and glory of the Roman law—
forgive me, Quintillian,
if I'm eager to enjoy life,
poor as I am, before
I'm old and incapable of it.
We can't be quick enough
to enjoy life. Let the fellow
who wants to pile up more money
than his father or fill his rooms
with statues of his ancestors
wait as long as he wants. I'm happy
now, with a fireplace
and a house that isn't too elegant
to be smudged with a little smoke,
and a lively spring, and a yard
that's never mowed. Just give me
a fat slave and a wife
who's not too intellectual
and easy sleeping at night
and days without lawsuits.

# BOOK III

## III, ii

To whom would you like to be sent
as a gift, little book? You better hurry
and get yourself a protector
or you'll find yourself snatched away
into somebody's smoky kitchen
to wrap fried tunafish in
or twisted into a pepper-cone
or an incense-holder.

You'll fly to Faustinus' bosom?
That's wise. Now you can stroll about
rubbed all over with cedar-oil
and decorated at both ends
with bright colors and painted bosses,
wrapped in a soft purple cover
with your title glowing magnificently
in scarlet. With a protector
like Faustinus, you can even thumb
your nose at Probus the critic.

## III, iii

You hide your lovely face
under layers of black grease
but insult the water in the bathing-place
with your ugly body. Believe me,
the water-nymph herself, speaking
through me, advises you:
either show us your face, or wear
your tunic when you're bathing.

### III, vii

Bye-bye, you measly hundred
quadrantes the parboiled bath-attendant
used to distribute as a dole
to us exhausted hangers-on.
What can we do about it,
my starving friends, now the bounty
of our rich patrons is cut off?
No shilly-shallying! Demand
your salaries back, right now!

### III, viii

"Quintus loves Thais." "Which one?"
"The one-eyed one." Thais
has only one eye missing.
He's completely blind.

### III, ix

Cinna writes poems against me,
they say. But is it writing
if nobody reads his poems?

## III, x

Your father set up an allowance
of two thousand sesterces a month
for you, Philomusus—doled out
a little bit every day.

That's because tomorrow's beggary
always followed today's extravagance,
and your vices couldn't be supported
without a daily wage.

But when he died, he left you
sole heir to all his money.
Your father disinherited you,
Philomusus.

## III, xi

If your girl's name isn't Thais,
and she isn't one-eyed, Quintus,
what makes you think my couplet
was aimed at you? Sometimes
these things are significant.
I might have called her Thais
and meant Lais. But where's
the connection between Thais
and Hermione? I'll admit
your name's Quintus. Let's change
the name of the lover. If Quintus
won't have her, we'll let Sextus
be in love with Thais.

## III, xii

I'll admit you gave your guests
some fine perfumes yesterday,
but there wasn't anything to carve.
That's a new one: smelling pretty
while you starve. Being anointed
with nothing to eat, Fabullus—
isn't that what happens to corpses?

## III, xvii

A tart sent round the table
at the second course was so hot
it burnt everyone's fingers badly.
But Sabidus' gluttony burned
even hotter. Immediately
he puffed out his cheeks and blew on it
three or four times. The tart
was cooler, all right. You could handle it
with your fingers. But nobody wanted
to touch such a filthy thing.

## III, xx

Tell me, Muse, what's Canius Rufus,
my old friend, up to these days?

Is he writing down, for posterity,
the deeds of Claudius' time?
Or those the lying chronicler
attributed to Nero?
Is he imitating Phaedrus'
improper fables? or wantoning
in elegiacs? or frowning
in heroics? or writing tragedies
in the manner of Sophocles?

Or is he loafing at the poet's club,
telling off-color stories, full
of Attic wit? Or leaving there,
does he stroll in the portico
of Isis' temple, or measure,
step by step, the entire length
of the Argonaut's Portico,
or sit or walk on the Portico
of Europa, free from worry,
surrounded by boxtrees, warming
in the soft afternoon sun?

Is he soaking in the warm baths
of Titus or Agrippa
or the one shameless Tigellinus
built? Or is he resting
at Lucianus' country place,
or Tullius', or driving
to Pollius' charming house
at the fourth milestone? Or lazily
sailing across Lake Lucrinus
on his way to steaming Baiae?

"Do you really want to know what
your friend Canius is doing?
He's laughing, as usual."

## III, xxii

You spent twice thirty million
sesterces on your belly,
Apicius, and even then
had a full ten million left.
But refusing to put up
with such hunger and thirst, you drank
one final beakerful of poison.
Nothing you'd done, Apicius,
was more gluttonous than that.

## III, xxvi

You've got your estates, Candidus,
all to yourself, and your money
all to yourself. And you've got
gold plate and porcelain vases
all to yourself, and choice wines
from Massicus and Caecubum
aplenty, all to yourself.
You've got brains and ability
all to yourself. In short,
you've got everything in the world
all to yourself. Don't think
I'm trying to deny it.
But you've got a wife, Candidus,
who belongs to everybody.


## III, xxvii

You never invite me to dinner,
though you come to my place every time
you're asked. Still, I'd ignore it
if you weren't inviting others.
But you do. I guess we're both
to blame. How's that, you say?
Because I'm a damn fool, Gallus,
and you've got no sense of shame.


## III, xxxiv

I'll tell you why your name—
Chione, which means snow—
is and isn't appropriate.
You're cold, all right, but you're black.
You are and aren't Chione.

## III, xxxv

See these fish, beautifully carved
in relief by Phidias' skill.
Add water and they'll swim.

## III, xxxvi

The duties an untried friend,
brand new, owes his patron—these
you make me perform for you,
Fabianus: greeting you
bright and early every morning,
all goosepimples, or dragging
along behind your sedan-chair
through the thickest mud, or following
when you go to the Baths of Agrippa
at the tenth hour or later
when I'm all worn out, and besides
I do my bathing at the Baths
of Titus, a mile or more away.

Is this what I deserve
after thirty winters, Fabianus—
to be still a mere beginner
in your retinue? Is this
what I deserve, Fabianus,
when my toga, which I paid for
myself, has been worn threadbare
in your service? Don't you think,
by now, I've earned a vacation?

## III, xxxviii

Tell me, what brings you to Rome
so self-confidently, Sextus?
What are you after, and what
do you expect to find there?

"First of all, I'll plead cases
more eloquently than Cicero
himself. There won't be anyone
in the three forums to touch me."

Atestinus and Civis
(you know them both) pled cases,
but neither one of them took in
enough to pay the rent.

"Well, if nothing comes of that,
I'll write poems. When you hear them,
you'll say they're Vergil's work."

You're crazy. Wherever you look
you'll see Ovids and Vergils—all of them
shivering in their thin cloaks.

"Then I'll cultivate rich men."

That sort of thing has supported
maybe three or four. The rest
of the crowd are pale with hunger.

"What *will* I do? Advise me.
I'm determined to live in Rome."

Well, Sextus, if you're honest,
you'll be lucky to stay alive.

### III, xli

Carved on this drinking-bowl
by Mentor's hand, the lizard
is alive, and we're afraid
to touch the silver.

### III, xlii

Polla, you try to cover up
your wrinkles with powder and paint,
but you're only fooling yourself,
not me. A minor blemish
should simply show. If it's hidden,
we imagine it's even worse.

### III, xliv

Do you want to know why nobody
runs into you on the street
if he can help it, Ligurinus?
And why, the minute you show up
anywhere, there's a general exodus
and vast solitude surrounds you?
You're just too much of a poet—
a mighty dangerous fault.
No tigress raging at the capture
of her cubs—no basking snake
in the noonday sun—no deadly
scorpion is as frightening
as that. I ask you, who
can endure such hardships as these:
You read me your poems while
I'm sitting and while I'm standing.
You read while I'm travelling somewhere
and while I'm going to the toilet.
I fly to the baths. You buzz

in my ear. I go to the swimming-place,
but I'm not permitted to swim.
I hurry off to dinner. You stop me
on the way. I reach the table.
You rout me out while I'm eating.
Worn out, I sleep. You rouse me
while I lie there. Shall I tell you
what a terrible nuisance you are?
You're an honest, decent fellow—
quite harmless, Ligurinus—
but you scare me out of my wits.


## III, xlv

I don't know whether Apollo
really fled from Thyestes' table
and the meal set out on it.
But we fly from yours, Ligurinus.

Not that it isn't elegant
and set with magnificent dishes,
but how can we enjoy anything
in the world while you're reading your poems?

You don't have to feed me turbots
or two-pound mullets. You don't
have to give me mushrooms, even,
or oysters. Just stop reading!

### III, xlvii

There, where the aqueduct
rains down in heavy drops
as it crosses the Carpean Gate.
Where they wash the Phrygian Mother's
sacred knife in the Almo River.
Where the holy burial field
of the ancient Horatii turns green.
And where the smaller Hercules'
temple is jammed with worshippers.
That's where Bassus was travelling
in an overloaded carriage,
Faustinus—dragging with him
all the things that grow abundantly
in the fertile countryside.

There you'd see great cabbage-heads
and green onions of every kind
and ground-lettuce and beets
that are good for sluggish stomachs.
And a hoopful of fat thrushes
and a rabbit some hunting-dog
had caught and a sucking pig
too young to feed on beans.
Even his runner was busy
as he walked ahead of the carriage
carrying eggs wrapped in straw.

Was Bassus headed for the city?
On the contrary, he was going
to that place he calls his farm.

### III, xlix

You serve me Veientan wine—
watered—while you drink Massic
straight. I'd rather smell
your cup than drink my own.

### III, l

You invited me to dinner
for one reason and no other,
Ligurinus—to read me your poems.
I take off my shoes at the table.
Immediately a huge volume
is brought in with the salad and canapés.
Another is read while we wait
for the first course, and a third
before our dessert is served.
And you read us a fourth, and finally
a fifth book. Even boar's meat
is sickening if you offer it
to me too often. If you don't
turn over your awful poems
to the fishmongers, Ligurinus,
you'll find yourself eating your dinner
at home, alone, after this.

### III, li

When I praise your face, Galla,
or admire your legs and hands,
you always say "You should see me
with nothing on!" And yet
you'll never go bathing with me.
Surely it's not how *I* look
you're worried about, Galla.

### III, lii

You bought a house, Tongilianus,
for two hundred thousand sesterces.
But an accident in the city
(they're all too common) destroyed it,
and your friends subscribed a million.
Now I ask you, isn't it possible
they'll think you set fire to it
yourself, Tongilianus?

### III, liii

I can get along without your face
and your neck and hands and legs
and breasts and buttocks and thighs.
And not to belabor the matter
in detail, I can get along
without you altogether, Chloe.

### III, liv

Since I can't pay the price you're asking
of anyone who wants you, Galla,
it would have been a lot simpler
if you'd said "no" in the first place.

### III, lv

Wherever you go, we imagine
that Cosmus, the perfume man,
is going by. Or that quantities
of cinnamon oil are escaping
from a broken bottle. Gellia,
you shouldn't indulge yourself
in exotic nonsense like this.
Don't you realize that my dog
can smell sweet that way too?

### III, lx

When I'm invited to dinner
these days, I don't get paid
the way I used to. So why
don't you serve me the same dinner
you eat? You get oysters, fattened
in Lake Lucrine. I cut my mouth
sucking a mussel from its shell.
Mushrooms for you. Pig's fungus
for me. You're busy with turbot,
I with brill. You stuff yourself
with a golden turtledove's
fat rump. I'm served a magpie
that died in its cage. Why is it,
Ponticus, when I dine with you,
I dine alone? Now the dole's gone,
you owe me the courtesy
of letting me share your dinner.

### III, lxiv

They say crafty Ulysses
managed to escape the sirens
with their fatal attraction for sailors
(death made irresistible,
joy barbed with cruelty)—
whom nobody could resist
once he'd heard them. Well, I'm willing
to believe it. But I'll never
believe that he or anyone
could escape from Canius's
long-winded anecdotes.

### III, lxviii

Lady, this book was written
for you—up to this page.
What about the rest of it?
Who's it written for? For me.
This part is full of the baths,
the gymnasium, the stadium.
You'd better be leaving now.
We're about to strip, and you wouldn't
want to look at naked men!

At this point Terpsichore
lays aside all modesty.
She's drunk, after the wine
and roses, and doesn't know
what she's saying. Now she's talking,
not in cloudy figures of speech
but plain language, about that image
of Priapus Venus welcomes
proudly in her sixth month rites,
and the bailiff sets up in the middle
of the garden to frighten thieves,
and your well-brought-up young lady
peeks at between her fingers.

If I know you, you were just
putting down this little book,
bored with its tediousness.
But now you're reading it, page
by page, not missing a line.

### III, lxix

Since you write all your epigrams
in language that's perfectly chaste,
and no indecencies ever
get into your poems, I'm full
of admiration and praise.
No one writes more respectably
than you.  On the other hand,
I've never written a page
without some obscenities.

Let good-for-nothing young men
and easy-going girls read me—
and old lechers, and men in trouble
with their mistresses.  Your poems—
so worthy of respect, Cosconius,
such models of propriety—
are perfect reading for children
and innocent young girls.

### III, lxxvi

You're crazy about old women,
Bassus, and loathe young girls.
It isn't beauty that attracts you
but moribundity.
Isn't this madness, I ask you?
Isn't it a kind of perversion—
to be on fire with Hecuba
and impotent with Andromache?

## III, lxxvii

Neither mullets or gamebirds please you,
or rabbit or boar's meat, Baeticus.
And you don't like cookies or squares
of cake. You won't touch birds
shipped in from Libya or Phasis.
You stuff yourself with capers,
instead, and onions swimming
in stinking fishsauce, and slices
of overripe ham, and sprats,
and dry, salt tunafish.
You drink resinated wine
and scorn the good Falernian.
I suspect you've ruined your stomach
with debauchery, Baeticus.
Why else would you eat such garbage?

## III, lxxix

Sertorius never finishes
anything. He begins things.
I'll bet he can't even finish
what he starts in bed.

## III, lxxxii

Anybody who has the stomach
for being a guest of Zoilus
would be better off eating with whores
and drinking from Leda's cracked winejug,
cold sober.  I say it's more honest
and easier to stand.

Dressed in green and propped with pillows
of purple silk, he lounges
on a couch reserved for himself
and keeps his guests at a distance
with his elbows.  A servant stands
ready with a red feather,
to make him vomit, and toothpicks
of mastic-wood, while a concubine
stretched out on her back stirs breezes
with a green fan to cool his brow.

A boy with a myrtle-branch
keeps the flies off, while a masseuse
works his body over quickly
and skillfully, rubbing his limbs
with outspread, educated fingers.
A eunuch waits for a finger-snap
to help aim his drunken master's
drunken tool in the right direction
while he urinates discreetly.

But he himself, bending backwards
to the mob at his feet (mixed in
with lapdogs mouthing gooselivers)

tosses little gobbets of boarmeat
to his wrestlers and feeds his concubine
rumps of turtledove.  We're served
raw wine from rocky Liguria
or must that's been quickly fermented
in Massilian smokehouses.
He toasts his household fools
with cups of crystal or onyx
filled with Opimian nectar.

And while he's drenching himself
in the most expensive perfumes,
he passes around without blushing
a gold shell filled with the grease
the cheapest whores douse their hair with.
When he's nine-tenths full of wine
he passes out, and snores.
We lie there, under orders
to honor his grunts with silence,
and toast each other with head-nods.

That's the arrogant kind of treatment
we endure from this fellow Malchio.
And without a chance to retaliate,
Rufus.  What a first-class bastard!

## III, xciii

After three hundred consulates,
Vetustilla, you've got three hairs,
four teeth, a grasshopper's breast,
and the legs and skin-coloring
of an ant. Your forehead's more wrinkled
than a woman's dress, and your tits
hang down like spiderwebs.

Compared with those jaws of yours
the African crocodiles
have lady-like mouths. Ravenna's
frogs have a pleasanter croak,
and Atrian gnats sing more sweetly.
Your vision is like a nightowl's
in the daytime, and you smell
like a she-goat's raunchy husband.

You've got a half-starved duck's
rear end, and even an old Cynic
would admit himself defeated
by that bony thing between your thighs.
The bathman won't let you in
among the whores that do business
in graveyards till he's put out
his lantern. Winter hangs on
well into the month of August
with you, and a pestilent fever
wouldn't thaw out your frozen joints.

In spite of all this and the fact
you've buried two hundred husbands,
you've the nerve to be looking around
for another one, crazily trying
to find a man who can work up

a lust for your burned-out body.
But who wants to hoe rocks? And who
wants to marry and call you wife
when Philomelus was calling you
grandma yesterday? Anyhow,
if you insist your cadaver
still needs pawing, trundle out
Death's wedding-bed. It's the only
suitable one for your marriage.

We'll invite the body-burner
to lead in the bride with torches
from the funerals. Only torches
could warm up those ancient thighs.

# BOOK IV

## IV, iv

The smell of a swamp-bottom
after it's drained, or the vapor
from a raw sulphur spring,
or the stink of an old fish-pond
full of sea-brine, or a stale
he-goat mounting a she.
Or the tired army-boot
of an infantryman, or a fleece
double-died purple, or Jews
fasting on the Sabbath, or sighs
from the losers in a lawsuit,
or dirty Leda's oil lamp
when it gutters out, or the dregs
of wrestler's oil, or a fox
on the run, or a viper's nest.
I prefer the smell of all these,
Bassus, to the way you smell.

## IV, v

You're a good man but poor
and honest in heart and tongue,
Fabianus. What are you after
in coming to Rome? You haven't
the makings of a pimp or parasite.
You couldn't give false evidence
in a solemn voice against
the frightened defendants in a lawsuit
or seduce your best friend's wife
or letch after frozen old hags
or peddle non-existent influence
at court or rent yourself out
as a claque for Canus or Glaphyrus.
Then how will you make a living,
without a trade? "I'm trustworthy
and a loyal friend." That's nothing.
You'll never make yourself rich,
like Philomelus, that way.

## IV, viii

The first and second hours are spent
paying morning calls.  The third
sets the lawyers arguing.
Rome spends the fourth and fifth
in business of various kinds.
The sixth provides a siesta
for tired souls.  And the seventh
brings our working-day to an end.
The eighth and ninth are enough
for the oiled wrestlers.  The ninth
bids us rumple the dinner-couches
piled with pillows.  The tenth hour
is the hour for my little book,
Euphemus, when your care
sets out the ambrosial banquet,
and benevolent Caesar unbends
with heavenly nectar, holding
a small cup in his mighty hand.
That's the time to read him my trifles.
My Muse is much too timid
to present herself uninvited
to a busy morning Jove.

## IV, x

While my little book is brand new—
its edges still unpolished
and its pages, not quite dry,
still capable of smudging—
go, boy, take this trifling present
to a dear friend who's entitled
to have the first look at my verses.
Hurry, but go provided.
I'm sending a Punic sponge
along with the book. It belongs
with a gift of this kind. My many
corrections may still leave errors.
This sponge will remove them all.

## IV, xv

Yesterday morning you asked me
to lend you a thousand sesterces
for a week or so, Caecilianus.
I told you I didn't have them.
But now, on the grounds that a friend
has come for a visit, you're asking
to borrow my silver dishes
and some vases. Are you stupid?
Or am I the one that's stupid—
you think? My friend, I refused you
a thousand sesterces. Why
should I give you five thousand now?

## IV, xvii

You're after me to write verses
against Lycisca—to make her
blush and go into a rage
when she reads them. You're a sly one,
Paulus. You want to fix it
so she'll sleep with nobody but you.


## IV, xix

I'm sending you as a gift
this garment with a Spartan name.
It's called an "endromis"—a thick,
shaggy homespun, woven in Gaul,
unstylish, but not to be despised
in this cold December weather.
Whether you're rubbing yourself
with wrestler's oil, or warming up
playing catch, or grabbing the ball
in a dusty game of scrimmage,
or batting the light-weight bladder-ball
back and forth with your arms and hands,
or trying to beat speedy Athas
in a race—the penetrating cold
won't get at your sweaty limbs
and Iris won't leave you half-drowned
from a sudden shower. You'll laugh
at winds and rainstorms, covered
with this gift I'm sending. You wouldn't
be nearly as well protected
in a purple linen gown.

## IV, xxi

"There aren't any gods. Heaven
is uninhabited," says Segius.
And he proves his point. While he's saying this,
he's getting richer and richer.

## IV, xxvi

Shall I tell you, Postumus,
what it's cost me not to pay
my morning calls at your place
for a whole year? Twice twenty,
or maybe three times twenty
sesterces. Please forgive me,
Postumus, but a cheap toga
costs me more than that.

## IV, xxviii

You've given young Lupercus
Spanish cloaks, dyed purple and red,
and a toga washed in the gentle
Galaesus River, and Indian
sardonyxes, and emeralds
from Scythia, and a hundred
newly minted gold coins,
and anything else he asked for,
again and again, Chloe.
Poor woman, you've lost your mind
over a smooth-skinned boy.
Your Lupercus will strip you naked.

## IV, xxix

I hurt my poems, Pudens,
my friend, by publishing
such mobs of them. So many
volumes weary the reader
and jade his appetite.
People like things that are scarce.
Early apples taste better,
and winter roses command
a higher price. The arrogance
of a mistress who takes all your money
makes her attractive. A door
that's always open won't keep in
a lover. And often a poet
like Persius gets more readers
with a single book than Marsus
with his epic about the Amazons,
spread thin over many volumes.
You too, whichever book of mine
you read again—pretend
it's the only one. That way
it will mean a lot more to you.

## IV, xxx

Fisherman, stay away
from that lake at Baiae, I warn you,
or you'll get yourself in trouble.
Those waters are stocked with holy fish
who recognize their master
and kiss that hand that's mightier
than any on earth. Each one
has a name and comes when he hears
his master's voice. Not long ago,
an irreverent Libyan
was pulling his catch from its depths
on a trembling string when his eyes
were snatched out in sudden blindness,
and he couldn't see the fish he'd caught.
Now he hates his cursed hooks
and sits by that lake at Baiae
begging. But you, while you can,
leave the place before you're in trouble.
But first, throw in your bait,
without hooks. Respect the Emperor's
pet fish.

## IV, xxxiii

Though you've boxes full of verses,
all finished, Sosibianus,
you publish nothing. Why?
"My heirs will bring out my poems,"
you say. But when? We can hardly
wait, Sosibianus,
for the chance to read your verses.

## IV, xxxvi

"Coranus owes me a hundred
thousand sesterces, and Mancius
two hundred thousand. Titius
owes me three hundred thousand,
and Albinus twice that much.
Sabinius owes me a million,
and so does Serranus. My farms
and tenements bring me in
three million, and my flocks
in Parma six hundred thousand."

You recite this to me, Afer,
every day, all day, and I
know it better than my own name.
But you'll have to count out something
for *me,* so I can stand it,
and cure my daily nausea
with cash. I can't go on
listening to all that money
of yours, Afer, for free.

## IV, xxxviii

Say no, Galla. Love is boring
if its joys aren't mixed with suffering.
But Galla, don't say no
too long.

## IV, xli

Why do you wear a muffler
around your neck when you're reciting?
We need it for our ears.

## IV, xliv

This is Vesuvius—green
until now with the vines' shadows.
Here excellent grapes loaded down
the dripping wine-presses.
Bacchus loved these mountains better
than Nysa's hills, and the Satyrs
held their dances here till recently.
Venus lived here and preferred it
to Sparta. And Hercules
made the place famous with his name.
Now everything's buried in fire
and funeral ashes. The proud gods
might be sorry they had such power.

## IV, xlix

Believe me, Flaccus—anyone
who calls epigrams mere trifles
and frivolities doesn't understand
what they are.  It's more frivolous,
really, when somebody writes
about Tereus' revolting dinner
or that undigestible meal
of yours, Thyestes, or Daedalus
fitting the meltable wings
to his son, or Polyphemus
grazing his Sicilian sheep.
That kind of windiness
won't be found in any of my poems.
My Muse doesn't puff herself up
with such tragic nonsense.

      "Still,
everybody praises that kind
of thing—admires it—worships it!"

Granted.  They praise it, but
it's my kind of poem they read.


## IV, liv

You've had the good luck to win
first prize in the Tarpean Games
for poetry—the gold oak-leaves.
They're circling your head right now,
deservedly, Collinus.

But now, if you're wise, you'll make
the most of each day as it comes—
as though you thought it were your last.
No one yet has ever persuaded
the three wool-spinning virgins
to change their minds. They never
waver from the fatal day.
You could be richer than Crispus—
as brave as Thrasea himself—
as distinguished as elegant Melior—
and Lachesis wouldn't add an inch
to the measured thread. She unwinds
the sisters' spindle, and one of them
stands ready to cut it.


## IV, lvi

Do you really expect me to call you
generous, Gargilianus,
just because you give handsome presents
to old men and widows without children?
There's nothing more sordid, and no one
more unscrupulous than you,
pretending your bribes are gifts.
It's like those deceitful hooks,
so attractive to greedy fish,
or the crafty bait we entrap
stupid wild animals with.
If you don't know already, I'll tell you
what true generosity is,
and what giving is, Gargilianus:
be generous to me.

## IV, lxi

The other day, Mancinus,
feeling proud and pleased with yourself,
you were boasting that a friend
had presented you with a gift
of two hundred thousand sesterces.
And when we were talking together
at the poets' club three days ago,
you told me your cloak—a gift
from Pompella—had cost ten thousand.
And you swore that Bassa and Caelia
had given you a real sardonyx,
with three separate stripes, and a pair
of aquamarines like sea-waves.

Then yesterday, leaving the theater
where Pollio was singing—
while you were hurrying away,
you said three hundred thousand
had come to you in a will,
and this morning you added a hundred
thousand, and this afternoon
a hundred thousand to that.

What have we ever done to you—
your friends? Take pity on us,
you cruel fellow. Stop talking
about such things all the time.
Or if you can't hold your tongue,
please tell us, once in awhile,
something we'd like to hear.

## IV, lxiv

Julius Martial's acres—they're few,
but more happily situated
than the gardens of the Hesperides—
lie along the sweeping ridge
of the Janiculum. Broad
ravines slope upward to the summit,
and the level, gently swelling top
opens to an untroubled sky
which shines with a light peculiarly
its own, even when cloudiness
obscures the curving valleys.
The dainty roof of the tall house
rises gracefully toward the clear stars.

On one side you can look out
on the seven proud hills and survey
the whole city of Rome, and the Alban
Hills and the hills of Tusculum,
and the cool suburbs nearby
the city: ancient Fidenae
and tiny Rubrae and the orchard
groves where Anna Perenna's
worshippers revel in the sacrifice
of maidenheads.

       On the other
we can see the traveller driving
along in his silent carriage
on the Via Flaminia
or the Salarian highway.
His wheels can never disturb
our soothing sleep, which neither
the calls to the rowers or the cries
of the bargemen are strong enough

to break, though the Mulvian Bridge
and the boats as they glide so swiftly
on the holy Tiber seem so near.

The owner offers his country house
(if it shouldn't be called a town house)
freely to guests. You'd think
it was yours, it's open to you
so courteously and ungrudgingly—
with such gracious hospitality.
You'd think it the friendly house
of Odysseus' host, Alcinous,
or that of Molorchus, just after
Hercules repaid his kindness
with sudden prosperity.

But if you're the kind who thinks
all this still isn't big enough,
you're welcome to farm the whole town
of Tibur, or even Praeneste,
with a hundred hoes, or assign
the hillside town of Setia
to one overseer. For me
Julius Martial's few acres
are preferable to them all.

## IV, lxvi

You've always lived a country life,
Linus, and there's nothing cheaper
in the whole world than that.

On the Ides and sometimes the Kalends
you shake out your well-worn toga,
and one dinner-gown has lasted you
ten summers.  The forests provide you
with boar-meat, the fields with rabbits
that cost you nothing, and the woods,
when beaten, yield fat thrushes.
Your fish are caught in the pools
of nearby rivers, and the wine
you pour out from your red wine-jar
didn't come from very far away.

You don't import expensive slaves
from Greece. A country crowd
stands around your rustic fireplace.
And whenever, heated with wine,
you feel the stirrings of passion,
you indulge it in the embrace
of some rough farmer's wife
or your own housekeeper's.

No fire has destroyed your house,
or Dog-Star brought sterility
to your fields. No ship of yours
has been lost at sea (there isn't
any ship of yours afloat.)
And you've never allowed the dicebox
to tempt you from old-fashioned gambling
for nuts with knuckle-bones.

Where did it go—that million
your miserly mother left you?
Did it simply vanish, Linus?
If so, you're a magician.


## IV, lxix

It's true you always serve Massic
or Setine wines, Papylus.
Yet rumor has it there's something
not quite right about them. They say
your wine-jug has made you a widower
four times. I can't believe it.
I'm sure it's not true, Papylus.
But all the same, I'm not thirsty.


## IV, lxxi

Safronius Rufus, I've looked
all over the city all day
for a girl who says "No." There aren't
any girls who say "No." Just as if
it was wrong, somehow, or disgraceful,
or against the law to say "No,"
there aren't any girls who say "No."

Does that mean there aren't any girls
who are chaste? There must be thousands.
Then what does a chaste girl do?
She manages to put them off,
but she never, never says "No."

### IV, lxxii

You beg me to give you my books,
Quintus. I haven't any,
but Tryphon the bookseller has.

"What, *buy* your poems, and spend
good money on trifles? I haven't
lost my mind. I wouldn't do anything
so foolish."

> Neither will I.

### IV, lxxxi

After she'd read my epigram
complaining there aren't any girls
who say "No" anymore, Fabulla
rejected her lover's entreaties,
though he begged her, not just once,
but twice, and even three times.
Give the poor fellow a chance,
Fabulla! I wanted you
to say "No," but I didn't expect you
to go on saying it forever.

### IV, lxxxv

While we drink from glass, you're drinking
from alabaster, Ponticus.
Why's that? A cup we could see through
might give it away that you're serving
two different kinds of wine.

## IV, lxxxviii

The five days of Saturnalia
are past, and you've sent me nothing
in return for my small present.

You might at least have given me
six scruples of cheap silver plate,
or a napkin some grumbling protegé
gave *you,* or a jar of fish-sauce
dyed red with Antipolitan
tuna fish blood.  Or one
full of tiny Syrian figs,
or an undersize basketful
of shrivelled Picenian olives,
just so you'd be able to say
you hadn't overlooked me completely.

Sweet words and that smiling face
may still fool others—not me!
I know a false friend when I see one.


## IV, lxxxix

Enough, little book.  Enough.
That's plenty.  We've come to the end
of the roll, but you want to go on
forever, and never stop talking,
even on the final page.
You think your work isn't done,
but to tell the truth, it was finished
back on page one.  The reader
is grumbling and putting you down
already, and even the copyist
is muttering to himself
"Enough, little book.  That's enough."

# BOOK V

## V, ii

Ladies, boys, and little girls—
this book's dedicated to you.
You others, who get so much fun
out of downright lasciviousness
and naked wit, read my four
improper books. This fifth one
was written to please the Emperor.
It's one Domitian can pick up
and read with virgin Athena
looking on—and never blush.

## V, viii

The other day, at the theater,
all aglow in his purple mantle,
Phasis was seconding the edict
of Domitian, our god and master,
which restored to members of the knighthood
their proper rank and established
rules for seating at public spectacles.
Full of pride and pompous language,
he was boasting: "Finally
the dignity of a gentleman
has been given back to him.
Now we can sit here in comfort
and not be contaminated
and crushed to death by the mob!"
Leaning back, he was uttering
these and similar pronouncements,
when Leitus, the seating attendant,
commanded the arrogant fellow—
purple cloak and all—to stand up.

## V, ix

When I wasn't feeling well, Symmachus,
you came immediately
with a mob of a hundred internes
to look me over.  A hundred
icy hands laid hold of me.
When I called you, Symmachus,
I didn't have any fever,
but I have one now.


## V, x

"Why is it, I wonder, that fame
never comes to living poets,
and most readers don't like anything
if it's written in their own day?"

You shouldn't be surprised, Regulus.
Envy always works that way—
preferring the ancient writers
to the new ones every time.
Thus we grieve, unreasonably,
for Pompey's old-fashioned portico,
and the gaffers will never stop praising
that ugly temple of Jupiter
Catulus restored.  When Vergil
was still alive, everybody
in Rome was reading Ennius,
and even Homer was laughed at
by his own generation.  Menander
got grudging applause in the theater
when he wore the laurel crown,

and only Corinna, his mistress,
thought Ovid amounted to much.

Don't be too eager, little books
of mine. I'm in no hurry,
if I can't be famous till I'm dead.


## V, xiii

I'll admit I'm poor, Callistratus,
and always have been. And yet
two Emperors gave me a knighthood
and I'm not altogether unknown,
and my reputation isn't bad.

I've got a great many readers
everywhere in the world who will say
"That's Martial," and recognition
such as few receive after they're dead
has come to me while I'm alive.

On the other hand, your house-roof
is supported by a hundred columns,
and your money-boxes contain
a freedman's wealth, and wide fields
near Syene on the River Nile
call you master, and Parma in Gaul
shears its countless flocks for you.

That's what we are, you and I.
But you can never be what I am,
while anyone at all can be like you.

## V, xiv

Nannius, in the old days
when anyone could sit where he pleased,
always grabbed a front-row seat.
It's different now.  Being routed
two or three times and compelled
to pitch camp in some other place,
he squats himself down behind Gaius
and Lucius, between two seats
as though he were sitting in a third one.
And there, with his head covered up
with his hood, he's peering out,
watching the show uncomfortably
with one eye.  Being driven out
from that place too, the poor fellow
moves out in the aisle and balances
himself at the end of a bench-row,
awkwardly, with one knee
bent to make it look to the gentleman
beside him as though he's sitting,
and the other straight, to make Leitus,
the seat-attendant, think he's standing.

## V, xv

This is my fifth book of trifles,
Augustus, and no one can complain
that my poems have done him any harm.
On the contrary, many a reader
has acquired undying fame
through my efforts, and takes pleasure
in the honor added to his name.

"But what is there in them for you,
however much honor they bring
to the others?"

Nothing tangible,
but I've had fun writing them.


## V, xvi

It's your fault, dear friend and reader,
that I write for your entertainment
when I might be using my talents
for something more serious.
You read my poems and sing them
all over Rome. Do you know
how much our friendship costs me?

If I decided to plead cases
in scythe-bearing Saturn's temple,
or put my tongue up for sale
to the highest bidder in the law-courts,
many ships would bring me wine-casks
from Spain, and all kinds of money
would be dirtying my purse.

As it is, my book's a reveller
and guest at drinking-parties,
and my pages make everyone happy
for free. But our ancestors
weren't satisfied with praise.
The least a poet could expect
was a gift like the slave Alexis

Maecenas presented to Vergil.

"You write beautifully," you say.
"We love your poems, and we'll never
stop praising them."

      Hypocrites!
You'll make a lawyer of me yet.


       V, xviii

It's December—Saturnalia time—
when handkerchiefs and little spoons
are flying around, and wax candles
and writing-paper and withered
Damascus plums in pointed jars.
But I've sent you nothing for a present
except my little home-made books.
Don't think it's because I'm stingy
or discourteous. The truth is
I dislike the crafty politics
of measuring the gift to the receiver
to get something better in return.
Presents can be like fish-hooks.
Everybody knows how the trout's
taken in by the fly he gulps
so greedily. Quintianus,
a poor man shows his generosity
whenever he gives a rich acquaintance
nothing at all.

## V, xx

If I were permitted to enjoy
my days with you, without worry,
idling the time away—
both free to live as we'd like to,
dear Julius Martial—we'd never
give a thought to great men's houses
with their roomfuls of arrogant statutes
of ancestors, or concern ourselves
with lawsuits and dreary debates
in the forum.  A stroll or a drive,
instead, and plenty of talk,
and books, and the open fields,
and the porticos, and warm baths,
and cool springs—those are the places
for us—it's there we'd spend our time.
As it is, neither of us lives
a life of his own, and we feel
the good days passing and slipping
away from us—each one wasted
but added to our account.
We know how we ought to live.
Why do we put it off, then?

## V, xxi

Apollodotus, the professor
of rhetoric, always used to say
"Hello, Quintus" to Decimus
and "How do you do, Mr. Thin"
whenever he met Mr. Fat.
Lately he's got their names straight.
It shows what a man can accomplish
when he puts his mind to it, Regulus.
He wrote them down and memorized them.

## V, xxii

If I wasn't eager to see you
this morning, Paulus—and deserved
to find you in—may your house
on the Esquiline seem even farther
away than it is.  I live
near the Tiburtine column, where Flora's
rustic temple faces the ancient
temple of Jove.  I must climb
the steep uphill path from Subura
where the pavement is always dirty
and the steps are never dry.
And then I have to fight my way
through the long mule-trains you see
hauling marble blocks with their tangle
of ropes and pulleys.  What's worse,
after I've got there—worn out
from a thousand exertions—the doorman
informs me you're not at home.
That's all I get for my wasted
energy—and a toga
drenched with sweat.  It's hardly worth
all that trouble to *see* you, Paulus,
in the morning.  If you're busy
paying morning-calls yourself,
you really can't expect such courtesies
from your friends.  Unless you'll stay
in bed till I get there, Paulus,
you can't be a patron of mine.

## V, xxiii

You used to wear drab-colored clothing,
Bassus, as long as no attention
was paid to the seating regulations
in the theater.  But lately
our benevolent Censor's concern
in such matters has led him to order
their revival, and genuine knights
are sitting wherever Oceanus,
the seating attendant, tells them to.
Now you're always dolled up in robes
dyed purple or flaming red,
as though you expected to deceive him
that way.  But there aren't any robes
worth the four hundred thousand sesterces
it takes to make a knight, Bassus.
If there were, my old friend Cordus
would have had his knighthood long ago.

## V, xxvi

"A-1 in cloak-wearing"—
that's what I called you, Cordus,
once when I was cracking jokes
in several of my poems.
But if, for some reason or other,
that annoys you, you can call me
"B-2 in wearing togas."

## V, xxviii

Nothing you could do, Aulus,
would make Mamercus speak of you
with kindness or think well of you.
You could surpass the Curvii
in brotherly love, or Nerva
in gentleness, or the Rusos
and the Macri and the Maurici
in courtesy and decency
and uprightness—or the Reguli
in rhetoric, or the Pauli
in wit. He'd gnaw at all of it
with his rotten teeth. Perhaps
you'll dismiss him as a spiteful fellow.
But I can't help pitying a man
who never likes anyone.

## V, xxxii

Crispus, in his last bequest,
didn't leave his wife a penny.
Then who was his beneficiary,
Faustinus? Crispus himself.

## V, xxxiv

Fronto, my father, and mother
Flacilla, I commend this girl
to you—my little sweetheart,
my darling, my tiny Erotion.
I don't want her to be frightened
by Tartarus' black shadows
and Cerberus' gaping mouth.
She'd have completed only six
cold winters if she had lived
that many days more. Let her play
beside such venerable guardians
like a child, and babble my name
with her childish tongue. And may
hard clods not cover her soft bones,
nor you, earth, press too heavily
upon her. She didn't on you.

## V, xxxix

Thirty times in a single year
you've changed your will, Charinus,
and each time I've sent you cakes
soaked in honey flavored with thyme.
I'm broke. Take pity on me,
Charinus, and change your will
less frequently, or accomplish,
once and for all, what that lying
cough of yours is always promising.
I've emptied my purse and my money-bags,
and even if I'd been wealthier
than Croesus, I'd still be poorer
than the poorest beggar, Charinus,
if I'd fed you nothing but beans
as many times as that.

## V, xlii

A clever thief might break into
your money-box and steal your silver.
Or a ruthless fire might destroy
the family home. Or a debtor
might cheat you out of your capital
as well as the interest.
Or sterile plowlands might fail
to return the seed-corn you planted.
Or an unscrupulous girl-friend
might get her hooks into the fellow
who looks after your money. Or sea-waves
might sink your ships full of goods.
It's only what you give your friends
that's beyond the vicissitudes
of fortune. You can keep anything
forever if you give it away.

## V, xliii

Thais's teeth are black,
Laecania's white as snow.
The reason? One has store-teeth.
The other wears her own.

## V, xliv

What's happened, all of a sudden,
I wonder? When I asked you,
Dento, four separate times,
to dinner (who would believe it?)
you dared to say "No." What's more,
when I'm following you, you never
look back, but go running away—
from *me,* whom you used to be looking for
in the baths and the theaters
and everywhere people were gathering.
That's the way it is. You've been captured
by a richer table. An ampler
kitchen's seduced you, you dog!
But soon—and it won't be long—
when you've been found out and rejected,
and the more expensive dining-rooms
won't put up with you anymore—
you'll come sniffing around the old bones
of the dinners I used to provide.

## V, xlvii

Philo swears he never dines at home.
And it's true. When no one invites him
to dinner, he doesn't eat at all.

## V, xlix

When I happened to see you just now,
sitting in the theater,
I mistook your solitary self
for three fellows, Labienus.
I counted your bald head wrong.

You've got hair on this side, and hair
on that—enough to do credit
to a boy.  But in between
your head's naked.  There isn't
a single hair to be seen
in that broad expanse.

You profited
from a similar misconception
last December, when the Emperor
was distributing box lunches
for the Saturnalia.  You came
back home with three baskets of bread.

I imagine three-headed Geryon
looked something like that, and I warn you:
don't go strolling past all those statues
in Philippus' portico.
If Hercules sees you, you're a goner!

## V, 1

Whenever I eat dinner at home,
Charopinus—without inviting you—
right away, you're my worst enemy.
And if you happened to discover
my kitchen fires had been started
without you, I'm sure you'd be ready
to run me through with your sword.
Can't I ever eat dinner in private,
even once? Nothing's more persistent
than this greed of yours, Charopinus.
From now on, I beg you, quit spying
on my kitchen, and let my cook,
just once, put one over on you!

## V, lii

Of course I remember the kindnesses
you've done me. I'll never forget them.
Then why don't I talk about them,
you ask? Because you do the talking,
Postumus. Every time I start
to tell anybody what you've done,
he says "Postumus told me that,
himself." But there are some things
that just don't come off very well
when both of us do them. One's
enough for this kind of job.
If you want me to tell the whole world
about it, keep quiet yourself.
Believe me, Postumus, kindnesses,
however great, lose their luster
if they're chattered about too freely
by the person who did the favor.

## V, liv

My friend the rhetoric professor
has taken to extemporizing.
He said hello to Calpurnius
without writing his name down first.

## V, lvi

You've been wondering and worrying
and asking me every day
whom you ought to hand over your son to
for instruction, Lupus.  I warn you:
stay away from all those grammarians
and professors of rhetoric.

Don't let him have anything to do
with Cicero's writings, or Vergil's,
and let Tutilius, the author
and advocate, earn his reputation
somewhere else.  If the boy writes poems,
disown the young versifier!

Does he want to learn to make money?
Then have him take lessons in harping
or fluting.  Or if the young fellow's
not too bright, you can turn him into
a salesman or an architect.

## V, lviii

"I'll begin really living—tomorrow."
You're always saying "tomorrow,"
Postumus. But that tomorrow
of yours—will it ever come?
How long will we have to wait
for your tomorrow, Postumus,
and where is it? Whereabouts
shall we look for it? Is it hiding
somewhere among the Armenians
or the Parthians? Your tomorrow
is already as ancient as Priam,
or Nestor, rather. Your tomorrow—
tell me, how much would it sell for
in the market today? You tell me
you'll begin really living tomorrow.
But perhaps it's already too late,
today. A wise man, Postumus,
would have started living yesterday.

## V, lix

I haven't sent you any gold
or silver plate. I'm doing this
for your sake, Stella, my friend
and poet. Anyone who gives
expensively counts on expensive
gifts in return. But these pots
of mine will let you off lightly.

## V, lxi

Who's that fellow with all the curls
that's hanging around your wife,
Marianus? That fellow whispering
in the lady's tender little ear
and leaning his elbow on her chair—
with those curls and those lady-like rings
on all his fingers, and his legs
plucked clean of every single hair.
Who is he? Why don't you tell me?

"He manages some business matters
for my wife," you say. Why, of course!
You can tell by his face he's a businessman—
a solid, no-nonsense fellow.
That ladies' man Aufidius
from Chios wasn't any sharper
in business matters than he is.

Poor Marianus, you deserve
to be slapped around by Latinus,
like Panniculus in the pantomimes.
I think you ought to take his place.
You say he looks after some business
for your wife. That curly fellow?
It isn't your wife's business
he's attending to. It's yours.

## V, lxiv

Pour me out a double bumper
of Falernian, Callistus.
And you, Alcimus, dissolve
a bit of summer snow in it.
Pour ointments unsparingly
till my hair drips with perfume.
Weigh my temples down with chaplets
of roses. Augustus' tomb
over there warns us to live
while we can, reminding us
the gods themselves can die.

## V, lxx

Perched on bar-stools in the vicinity
of the four public bathing-places,
Syriscus, that hair-brained fellow,
ran through the full ten million
some patron had showered upon him
not long before. How's that
for gluttony, Maximus?
Eating up ten million! And doing it,
what's even more amazing, without
sitting down to a decent meal.

## V, lxxvi

By drinking poisons every day,
Mithridates made himself immune
to the deadly drugs. You've taken
precautions too, by dining
so poorly every day, Cinna,
that hunger can never kill you.

## V, lxxviii

If you're bored with lonely dinners
at home, Toranius, come starve
yourself at my table. You won't
have to do without appetizers,
if that's what you're accustomed to:
I've plenty of coarse Cappodocian
lettuce, and strong green onions,
and chunks of tuna fish, garnished
with egg-slices. Next we'll have
green broccoli, freshly picked
from my cool garden and served
on black earthenware plates—so hot
you'll scorch your fingers eating it—
and sausages wrapped in batter
as white as snow, and yellow beans,
and red bacon. And if you favor
a dessert to top things off with,
you can have your choice of raisins,
and pears that are said to come
from Syria, and chestnuts grown
by the clever Neapolitans
and toasted on a slow fire.
You'll add distinction to the wine
by drinking it. And after that,
if Bacchus, as he usually does,
stirs up a second appetite,
choice olives recently harvested
from Picenian trees will relieve it—
and roast lupins and chick-peas.

I won't pretend my little dinner's
impressive, but you can relax
and wear your natural expression
and not have to stand on ceremony
while you're talking or listening.
And your host makes a solemn promise
not to read from a fat manuscript
of his poems and not to assault you
with cheap dancing girls from Spain
waggling their lascivious thighs
in the same old bumps and grinds.
Instead, Condylus will play
something not too lugubrious
and dull on his little flute.

So much for my dinner. Oh yes,
I almost forgot. Claudia
will be there too. What more
can you ask of me than that!


### V, lxxxi

If you're poor, Aemilianus,
you always will be. Nobody
gets richer nowadays
unless he's rich already.

### V, lxxxiv

Leaving his toys unwillingly,
the schoolboy's going back to school
at the strong-voiced teacher's call.
And the drunken gambler, betrayed
by the rattling of his dicebox
with its illegal fascination
and dragged from his cozy tavern,
is pleading with the Aedile.
The Saturnalia's all over,
Galla, and you haven't sent me
the slightest thing for a present—
not even something less expensive
than you usually do.
Well, let it go—my December.
But your holiday's coming, Galla,
I suppose you know, when the first
of March brings the Matronalia.
When that time comes, I'll be giving you
exactly what you gave me.

# BOOK VI

## VI, v

I bought myself a country place
at a stiff price, Caecilianus,
and I'm hitting you up for a loan
of a hundred thousand.
　　　　No answer?
I suppose that means you're saying
to yourself "He'll never pay it."
That's exactly what I was thinking,
Caecilianus, when I asked.

## VI, xiv

You keep insisting, Labierus,
that you know how to write fine poems.
Then why is it you're unwilling
to try? Knowing how to write
fine poems and never doing it!
What will power, Labierus!

## VI, xix

I'm not suing anybody
for assault and battery
or poisoning. It's only
those three goats of mine. I claim
my neighbor got them away from me
by trickery. That's the charge
the judge expects you to defend.

But you're speaking, in a great voice
and with every conceivable gesture,
about the Mithridatic Wars,
and Cannae, and the Carthaginians'
outrageous lies, and Sullas
and Mariuses and Muciuses.

Won't you say something, Postumus,
about those three goats of mine?

## VI, xx

I hit you up for a loan
of a hundred thousand sesterces,
Phoebus, after you'd said to me
"Isn't there something I can do?"
For ten days now you've been asking
questions, and hesitating
and putting it off, and tormenting
yourself and me. Please, Phoebus,
I'm asking you now. Say "No".

## VI, xxx

If you'd given me the six thousand
sesterces immediately
and told me "Take them, they're yours,
as a gift," I'd feel that I owed you
two hundred thousand, Paestus.
But now, when you give them to me
after so much waiting—some seven
months later, or is it nine?—
I'll tell you, if you want me to,
something truer than truth, Paestus.
Your six thousand are gone forever.


## VI, xxxi

You know your wife's playing around
with your physician, Charidemus,
but you don't do anything about it.
My guess is you won't have to wait
for a fever to carry you off.


## VI, xxxii

While Enyo, the civil war goddess,
hadn't yet made up her mind,
and gentle Otho might have won
a victory still, he cursed
all wars, with their extravagant
costs in blood, and stabbed himself
with a deliberate hand.
If we grant that Cato, living,
was even greater than Caesar,
wasn't Otho, in the way he died,
a better man than Cato?

## VI, xli

That fellow reading his poems
with a woollen scarf around his neck
up to the chin—it's obvious
he's in no condition to speak
and yet he won't keep still.

## VI, xlii

If you don't try the baths at Etruscus
you'll never know what bathing is,
Oppianus.  No other bathing-place
is quite so pleasant—not even
the springs at Aponus, where women
aren't allowed, or soothing Sinuessa,
or the steaming waters at Passer,
or elegant Anxur, or the pools
at Cumae, or famous Baiae.

Nowhere else does the cloudless sunshine
fall so lazily.  The hours
of daylight seem longer there
and there's no other place where the days
linger so, as they go by.
Green marble from Taygetus
is blended very handsomely
with the finest particolored stone
from Phrygia and Libya.
The rich onyx radiates
dry heat, and the snake-stone glows
with a warmth peculiarly its own.

If it's Spartan baths you prefer
you can rest yourself in the drying-room
before plunging in the pure water

where the aquaducts of Marcia
and the Virgin meet—it's so clear
and bright and unclouded, you'd think
there wasn't any water there,
but only the empty channel
of white Lygdian marble you see.

You're not really paying attention,
but are listening all this time
with your ear half asleep, as though
you were bored with the whole matter.
Listen, or you'll never know
what real bathing is, Oppianus.


## VI, xliii

While you're indulging yourself,
Castricus, at charming Baiae—
bathing in its pleasant spring
of white water tinged with sulphur—
just loafing on my little farm
at Nomentum (with its house
not too big for the surrounding fields)
restores me. This is my Baian
sunshine, my Lucrine lake,
soothing and gentle—my equivalent
of the elegance you're enjoying,
Castricus. Once upon a time
I cheerfully hurried here and there
to the famous bathing-places.
No trip was too long for me to take.
But now it's places near the city
that attract me, and quiet retreats
easy to get to. It's enough,
for me, just being lazy.

## VI, xlviii

This crowd in their dinner-clothes
cheering you with loud cries
of "Bravo"—it's not your eloquence
that moves them, Pomponius,
it's your dinner.

## VI, l

In the days when Telesinus moved
in a circle of respectable friends,
he went around shabby and poor
in a toga that didn't keep the wind out.
Then he started associating
with a crowd of shameless libertines.
Now he spends more money on silver
and dinners and real estate
than any one else. Do you want
to get rich, Bithynicus?
Join that gang. Respectable friendships
won't get you a single penny.

## VI, li

Since you're giving so many parties
without asking me, Lupercus,
I've figured out a way to get even.
I'm really sore about this.
Hereafter you can invite me,
and send for me, and beg me—

"What will you do?" you ask.

What will I do? I'll come.

## VI, lvii

You cover your bald pate
with greasy ointments, painted
to look like hair. You'll never
need a barber to give you a haircut.
What you need, Phoebus, is a sponge.


## VI, lix

Baccara grumbles and complains
if it isn't freezing weather.
That's because he's got so many
winter cloaks. He can hardly wait
for gloomy mornings, and winds,
and snow. Even winter days
don't suit him, if they're mild ones.

What harm has it ever done you,
you cruel fellow—this cloak
of mine that the slightest breeze
sets flapping about my shoulder-blades?
How much kinder and more honest
if you'd put on your winter cloaks
even in the middle of August.


## VI, lx

All Rome praises my poems,
and enjoys them, and repeats them.
I'm in everybody's pocket
or his hand. That fellow there—
he blushes and turns pale.
He's dazed. He yawns. Now he's angry.
That's the way I like it. Sometimes
my verses please even me.

## VI, lxiv

You're no scion of the Fabians'
stern race and bear no resemblance
to Curio's wife, who was taken
in labor while carrying his lunch
to her husband at the plow—
she gave birth under an oak tree.
On the contrary, you're the son
of a father who dresses his hair
in front of the mirror and a mother
who's a whore. And your own wife
can hardly remember you're a man.

And yet you criticize my poems,
which are famous, and think you're qualified
to disparage my amusing trifles—
those trifles to which, I may add,
the prominent men of the city
and the law courts aren't unwilling
to bend an attentive ear.
The immortal poet Silius
finds room for them among his books,
and Regulus, the advocate,
repeats them on many occasions
with his eloquent voice. And Sura,
with his close-up view of the contests
in the great Circus from his house
near Diana's temple on the Aventine,
speaks well of them. Caesar himself,
though he carries the burdens of empire,
deigns to look at them now and then.

Are you wiser than they? Did Minerva
hone your wits to a finer point
and the subtlest Athenian scholarship

form your taste? There's more wit and wisdom,
I'll bet my life, in the carcase
the blood-stained butcher goes carrying
through the streets, with its bloody guts
and huge feet and lungs hanging out—
rotten and stinking. And still
you have the nerve to attack me
in these stupid verses which no one
will read—a waste of the paper
they're written on. On the other hand,
if I should let the full heat
of my anger be branded upon you,
it will live on and cling to you
and be read all over the city,
and Cinnamus, the hair-dresser,
for all his remarkable skill,
couldn't cover up the scars.

Poor man, take pity on yourself
and don't let your raving tongue
tempt the anger of a living bear.
He might turn out to be gentle
and lick your fingers and hands,
but if annoyance and rage
and a proper resentment compel him,
he'll behave like a bear. Wear out
your teeth on some empty hide,
instead, or find a piece of meat
to chew on that won't bite back.

## VI, lxv

I can almost hear Tucca saying
"You wrote that last epigram
in hexameters!"
       That's common
enough. There's no law against it.

"But see how long it is!"
That too is permissible
and customary, Tucca.

If the only epigrams you like
are the shorter ones, don't read
anything but couplets. Let's
agree: you skip the long ones,
Tucca. Just let me write them.


## VI, lxx

After sixty years, Marcianus,
or even, I think, sixty-two,
Cotta can't remember going through
a single day of lying wearily
in bed with a fever. He thumbs
his nose at the doctors: Alcon
and Dasius and Symmachus.

As for us, if we reckon carefully
our years and subtract from the better ones
all those which violent fevers
and lassitude and racking pain
stole away, we're nothing but children,
though we seem old men. Anyone
who thinks Priam's life, or Nestor's,
was long is deceived, Marcianus,
and greatly mistaken. Life isn't
simply living. It's living well.

## VI, lxxi

She knew all about belly-dancing
to the rhythm of Spanish castanets.
She could writhe to those Spanish tunes
in a way to stir up the libido
of Peleus, trembling with age,
or old Priam at Hector's funeral.
Now Telethusa's got her master—
that was—on fire and in torture
with love. She was a slave-girl
when he sold her. She'll be his mistress
now he's buying her back again.

## VI, lxxiv

That fellow over there, reclining
on the middle couch, with three hairs
plastered down in neat little rows
on his shiny pate—who's digging
at his ample jaws with a toothpick
of mastic—that fellow's a liar,
Aefulanus. He hasn't any teeth.

## VI, lxxxii

The other day a certain fellow
was looking me over so intently
you'd have taken him for a dealer
in slaves or a trainer of athletes,
Rufus. He stared at me
and pointed his finger and said
"Are you really Martial—the Martial
whose naughty poems everybody
knows by heart? Everyone, at least,
who hasn't got a tin ear?"

I smiled, modestly, and nodded
my head a little and admitted
I was the person in question.
"Then why," he said, "do you wear
such a threadbare cloak?" The only
answer I could think of was to say
"Because I'm a threadbare poet."

That sort of thing mustn't happen
to an author too often, Rufus.
Why not send me a decent cloak?

## VI, lxxxvi

Setine wine—glass after glass,
chilled with snow—when will my doctor
let me drink you again? Anyone
who'd rather inherit Midas' money
is a fool who doesn't know a good thing
when he sees it. He doesn't deserve
such a blessing. Let my worst enemy
corner all the harvests of Africa
and the gold from Spanish rivers—
and drink his wine-and-water warm.

## VI, xci

The sacred edict of our mighty chief
forbids adultery. Don't worry,
Zoilus. You're impotent.

## VI, xciii

Thais stinks. Worse than a stingy
fuller's old urine crock smashed
just now in the middle of the road.
Or a he-goat fresh from his lechery.
Or a lion's breath. Or the skin
peeled from a dog across the Tibur.
Or a chick when it's gone rotten
in an addled egg. Or a jug
poisoned with decaying fish-sauce.

Trying to cover up the smell
with other smells, she slyly
paints herself green with ointments,
or hides herself behind a coating
of chalk and vinegar, or plasters
herself with three or four layers
of bean-paste every time she strips
for the baths. But after a thousand
such tricks, and when she imagines
she's perfectly safe, Thais
(in spite of everything she does)
still stinks of Thais.

# BOOK VII

## VII, x

Eros is one kind of pervert,
Linus another. Agreed.
But what's it to you, Olus,
how either one of them conducts
himself? It's true Matho spends
a hundred thousand on a whore.
But what's it to you, Olus?
It's Matho who'll end up bankrupt
because of that, not you.
Sertorius goes on eating
and drinking till dawn. What's it
to you, Olus? You're free
to snore the whole night through.
Lupus is in debt to Titus
seven hundred thousand sesterces.
What's it to you, Olus?
You needn't give Lupus a penny,
or lend him one. You ignore
some things that are your business,
Olus, and more appropriate
for you to be worrying about.
You're in debt for that wretched toga.
That is your business, Olus.
So is this: no one will lend you
a dime nowadays. And your wife's
sleeping around. That's your business,
Olus. And this: that buxom
daughter of yours needs a dowry
right away. I could name fifteen
other things that are your business.
But whatever you're up to, Olus,
is really no business of mine.

## VII, xiv

An unspeakable calamity
has happened to my girl, Aulus.
She's lost her plaything, her darling.
Not such a one as Lesbia,
gentle Catullus' friend,
wept about when her pet sparrow's
naughty tricks were taken away from her.
Nor such as Ianthis, of whom
my Stella sings, lamented
when her black dove flew away
to Elysium.  My love
isn't caught up in such trifling
troubles as these.  Such losses
wouldn't break my mistress' heart.
She's lost a boy who was barely
twelve, but his equipment
was amazing for so young a fellow.

## VII, xvi

I haven't a penny to my name,
and there's only one thing I can do.
Those presents you gave me, Regulus—
I'll sell them.  Will you buy?

## VII, xvii

Charming country-house library,
from which the reader looks out
across the city, close at hand—
if there's any room for Thalia,
the merry Muse, among your sober,
more respectable poems (a pigeonhole
near the floor, perhaps) accept
these seven small books I've sent,

corrected in the author's hand.
Such scribblings will only make them
more valuable.  Take it
as a dedication—this little
present of mine, this pledge
of my affection—and guard it
well.  And may you be heard of
and talked about everywhere
in the world, Julius Martial's library!


## VII, xx

No one's a match for Santra
in miserliness or gluttony.
When he hurries to the fine dinner
he's spent his days and nights wangling
an invitation to, he asks
for three helpings of the boar's kidneys
and four of the loin, and both legs
and haunches of the hare.  He's never
ashamed to lie about the thrush
he claims he wasn't served, or steal
handfuls of bluish-bearded oysters.
He stains his well-spotted napkin
with mouthfuls of cake, and packs into it
grape jellies and bits of pomegranate
and the ugly skin of a sow's womb
scooped clean of what it was stuffed with,
and a half-eaten fig, and a mushroom
nibbled at the edges.  And when
his napkin's all ready to burst
with a thousand small pilferings,
he hides gnawed bones and the body
of a pigeon with its head chewed off
in the sweaty folds of his toga.

He doesn't think it's disgraceful
to sweep up whatever leavings
the household dogs have overlooked
with his long right arm. But stolen food
alone won't satisfy his greed.
He empties out all the wine-dregs
into a flagon out of sight
at his feet. And when the greedy fellow
has carried all these things home
up two hundred stairs to his garret
and locked himself in, safe and sound—
the very next day, he's around
offering the stuff for sale.


## VII, xxiv

Rumor-monger, if you're trying
to get me involved in a quarrel
with my good friend Juvenal,
there's no slander you wouldn't dare.
Your unscrupulous fantasies
might have persuaded Orestes
to turn against Pylades,
or diverted Theseus' love
from Perithous. You're capable
of estranging the Sicilian brothers,
Amphinomus and Anapius,
or Atreus' more famous sons,
Agamemnon and Menelaus,
or Leda's Castor and Pollux.
This is my curse on you,
you slanderer. This is what
such shameless effrontery deserves:
to go on the rest of your life
doing what you're doing now.

## VII, xxv

You always write epigrams
as sugary sweet and spotless
as a painted face, with never
a pinch of salt or a drop or two
of bitter gall in them. And yet,
you idiot, you expect
us to read them. Food itself
isn't palatable unless
it's seasoned with a touch of vinegar,
and a face isn't really attractive
without a dimple. Honey-apples
and insipid figs are for babies.
I prefer the Chian variety
that have a little tang to them.

## VII, xxx

You give yourself to Parthians
and to Germans and Dacians,
Caelia, and never refuse
to go to bed with Cilicians
and Cappadocians.
An Egyptian playboy comes sailing
from Pharos to sleep with you,
and so does a blackamoor
from somewhere around the Red Sea.
You don't spurn the lecheries
of circumcised Jews, and a Tartar
riding his Sarmatian steed
can stay with you. Why is it,
even though you're a Roman girl,
no Roman buck can satisfy you?

## VII, xxxvi

When my ramshackle country house
refused to stand up any longer
under Jove's torrential rains
and was swimming in the winter floods,
you provided me, in your kindness,
with rooftiles—enough to carry off
the sudden showers. But look
how December's roaring now
with the north wind's terrible howling!
You covered my farm, Stella.
How about covering the farmer?

## VII, xxxix

When he wouldn't put up any longer
with running here and there in attendance
on his patrons—or their arrogance
and condescension and those silly
morning-calls, Caelius
pretended that he had the gout.
And to make it seem more convincing
he smeared his healthy feet with greases
and wrapped them up in bandages
and hobbled around like a cripple.
But so great is the power of suggestion
in such matters, that Caelius
has given up pretending to suffer
from the gout. He's got it now.

## VII, xlvi

While you're trying to compose a poem
to go with the present you send me—
hoping to write something cleverer
than Homer's epics—you're keeping
yourself and me on the hot seat
day after day, Priscus.
Your Muse won't utter a word
and I'm as hard up as ever.
Save those verses and noble elegies
for fellows with plenty of money.
Hard cash is good enough for me.

## VII, xlviii

Though Annius has enough tables
for three hundred guests, more or less,
he uses waiters instead.
Dishes and courses come and go
as if they had wings. You can keep
that kind of banquet for yourselves,
you epicures! As for me,
I don't like eating on the fly.

## VII, li

If you don't want to pay good money
for my trifles, Urbicus,
but would like to make the acquaintance
of my naughty poems all the same—
go find Pompeius Auctus.
Perhaps you know him. He sits
in the temple of Mars the Avenger—
near the doorway, absorbed in the law
and a clever performer in the courtroom.

He isn't a reader of my book.
He's the book itself, Urbicus!
He knows my poems so well
he can recite them by heart
without missing a single letter
from the pages as I wrote them.
In fact, he could pass himself off
as the author, if he cared to,
but he'd rather boost my reputation,
instead. After four o'clock
(for he won't be finished with his work
till then) you can ask him to dinner—
a small one, for two. He'll recite.
You'll drink. He'll go on reciting,
whether you want him to or not.
Even when you say "That's enough!
Stop!" he'll keep on reciting.


## VII, liii

You've sent me, for the Saturnalia,
every present the five-day holiday
brought *you*, Umber: a dozen
three-leaved writing-tablets, and seven
toothpicks. These were accompanied
by a cup, a napkin, a sponge,
and half a peck of beans, together
with a wicker basket of olives
from Picenum and a black bottle
of new Laletanian wine.
Some small dried prunes came with them,
and a heavy jar, weighed down
with Libyan figs. Altogether
these presents of yours must have come
to thirty sesterces at the most,

but it took six hulking Syrians
to carry them.  How much easier
if a boy, with no effort at all,
had brought me five pounds of silver!

## VII, liv

You're always telling me, mornings,
the dreams you've been having about me
the night before.  It worries me
and keeps me upset.  I've exhausted
all the wine from last year's vintage
in libations—and this year's too—
while the witch-woman's exorcising
your dreams about me.  I've used up
mountains of barley and incense.
My flocks are dwindling away
with all the lambs I've sacrificed,
and I haven't a pig left,
or a hen, or even any eggs.
Either stay awake, Nasidianus,
or dream about yourself, for a change.

## VII, lviii

You've married six or seven fairies
already, Galla. You're a sucker
for long hair and a beard
neatly combed. And when you've discovered
how limp and worn out and impotent
they are (no amount of handling
will get them ready for the fray),
you give up these weaponless encounters
and lady-like husbands and try
again. But you always land
in the same old luke-warm bed.
Go find some fellow who's always
extolling the old Roman virtues
of the Curii and the Fabii—
some shaggy, wild-eyed fellow
that looks like a farmer. You'll find him
soon enough. But even that crowd
of sober-sides has its fairies,
Galla. A real man's hard
to get your hooks on, nowadays.

## VII, lxi

They were stealing the whole city—
those audacious shopkeepers.
There wasn't a single establishment
that didn't spill over its doorsill
into the streets themselves.
Now Germanicus has ordered
our narrow lanes to expand.
What used to be footpaths have turned
into proper streets. The doorposts
aren't festooned with bottles on chains
anymore. The praetors no longer

have to pick their way through the mudholes
in the middle of the road. We don't
have barbers brandishing their razors
at random in the tangled crowds.
And food-vendors can't monopolize
every inch of the pavement. The barber,
the butcher, the wineseller,
and the cook are kept in their places
inside their shops, and Rome,
which used to be one enormous
bazaar, is a city again.

## VII, lxv

One lawsuit in three lawcourts
has cost you twenty icy winters,
Gargilianus. Poor fellow,
you must be crazy. Would anyone
spend all those years of his life
on litigation? It's better
to let yourself lose, Gargilianus.

## VII, lxxii

Happy Saturnalia, Paulus.
I hope you'll be spared the usual
flood of worthless writing tablets
and bobtailed napkins and half-pound
packages of frankincense,
underweight at that. Perhaps,
instead, some important client
or rich acquaintance will bring you
silver dishes, or winecups, treasured
in his family for generations.
Or—you'd like this even better—
I hope you'll give Publius

and Novius a beating at chess,
hemming in their men with your pawns
and knights.  Or when you're playing
three-man handball, stripped to the waist,
perhaps the bystanders, watching
in a circle, oiled for the baths,
will admire your left-handed shots
more than Polybus' and decide
you're the winner.  But suppose
some bad-tempered fellow should try
to pass off his miserable poems
soaked with poison as mine: defend me
with a patron's voice.  Proclaim
at the top of your lungs without stopping:
"My Martial never wrote that!"

## VII, lxxiii

You've a house on the Esquiline
and a house on Diana's hill
and another in Millionaires' Row.
From this one you have a view
of widowed Cybele's shrine.
From that one of Vesta's.  From here
you look out on Jove's new temple.
From there you can see the old one.
Tell me, where am I expected
to call on you?  In what part
of the city shall I look for you?
A man who lives everywhere, Maximus,
doesn't live anywhere at all.

## VII, lxxxi

Thirty bad epigrams
in a whole volume, Lausus?
If you find that many good ones,
it's an excellent book.

## VII, lxxxiv

While my portrait for Caecilius
Secundus is still being painted
and the canvas is coming alive
under the painter's cunning hand,
go instead, my book, to Getic
Peuce and subjugated Ister,
which he rules, with their conquered tribes.
You'll make him a welcome gift—
my dear friend—however small.
He'll see my face even better
in my poems, which accident
and time's ravages can't destroy.
When the painting crumbles into dust,
the poems will still be alive.

## VII, lxxxv

You're to be commended, Sabellus,
for writing a number of quatrains
that aren't bad, and a few nice couplets.
That's really not so surprising.
It's easy enough to dash off
a decent epigram. The hard thing
is writing a book of them.

## VII, lxxxviii

They say my little books are cherished
among her dearest possessions
by beautiful Vienna, nestled
on the Rhone.  If the rumor's true,
every old man and younger man
and boy reads me there, and even
the modest bride in the presence
of her strait-laced husband.  This
pleases me more than if my poems
were chanted by the tribes that drink
from the Nile at its headwaters,
or if my own Tagus showered me
with Spanish gold, or if Hybla
or Hymettus fed my bees.
After all, I'm not unheard of
and haven't been deceiving myself
with the speeches of flattering tongues.
I think I believe you now,
Lausus, when you found only thirty
bad epigrams in my book.

## VII, xc

Matho tells every one I've written
an uneven book.  If that's true,
it's a compliment.  Calvinus
and Umber write books that don't vary
a hair's breadth from dull uniformity.
But variety's the spice of life
in books, too, Criticus.

## VII, xcii

"If there's anything I can do,
you know you don't have to ask."
You say this, two or three times
in a single day, Baccara.
Hard-fisted Secundus duns me
in an angry voice. You hear him,
Baccara, and can't imagine
what there is you can do for me.
I'm informed my rent is overdue—
loudly, with everyone listening
and you standing by. You hear it,
Baccara, and can't imagine
what there is you can do for me.
I complain that my cloak is threadbare
and won't keep me warm. You hear me,
Baccara, and can't imagine
what there is you can do for me.
You can do this: get struck
by lightning, suddenly, Baccara,
so you won't be able to keep saying
"If there's anything I can do. . . . ."

## VII, xciv

Just now, my little onyx box
contained perfume. Then Papylus
sniffed. Look, it's turned fishsauce!

## VII, xcv

It's winter, and raw December's
a cake of ice. Yet you venture
to greet everybody you meet,
here and there, with a frozen kiss.
You've embraced the whole city of Rome
by now, Linus. What crueller,
more terrifying revenge
could you take if you'd been beaten
and whipped? In this cold weather
not even my wife or little daughter
with her coaxing lips give me kisses.
Do you think you're so much more dainty
and appealing, with a blue icicle
hanging from your dog-like snout
and your ice-caked beard, as stiff
as the wool a Sicilian shearer
cuts from an African he-goat
with his upturned clippers? I'd rather
encounter a hundred perverts,
and I'm less afraid of a priest
of Cybele, recently unmanned.
I beg you, Linus, if you've any
decency or shame—put off
this wintry kissing until April.

## VII, xcviii

You buy everything in sight, Castor,
but you'll end up selling it all.

# BOOK VIII

## VIII, iii

"Five books were enough. Six or seven
are too many. Tell me, Muse,
why you want to carry on the game
so long. Enough's enough.
There's not another thing that fame
can give me now. My book
is in everyone's hands. And after
Messalla's tomb lies in ruins,
neglected, and the huge pile
of marble Lucinus erected
is dust, there will still be voices
to recite me. Many a stranger
will carry my poems back home
to his native land." I stopped,
and the ninth of the sisters—Thalia,
the Muse of epigram (her hair
and even her clothing drenched
with perfume)—gave me her answer
like this: "You ungrateful fellow.
Do you plan to give up the trifles
you've had so much fun with? What else,
may I ask, will you write that's better,
if you do? Are you thinking of swapping
your jokes for the mantle of tragedy,
or of thundering in hexameters
about violent wars, so a pompous
pedagogue with a raucous voice
can recite you, and buxom girls
and sturdy boys will learn to hate you?
Let those overly solemn, overly
grim fellows who slave till midnight
under the lamp write such things.

But you—dip your Roman pen
in light-hearted wit.  Let life
read an image of her own manners
and recognize it there.  You may sing
to a very small pipe, if your pipe
drowns out the trumpets of others."


## VIII, vi

Old Auctus, with his antique cups,
is the world's worst bore.  (I prefer
cheap mugs of Saguntine clay.)
He delivers a spurious pedigree
with each piece of silver, and sours
the wine with his endless prattling.

"These cups once graced Laomedon's
dinner table.  And to win these
Apollo built the walls of Troy
with his lyre.  Rhoetus the centaur
carried this very mixing-bowl
into the battle with the Lapiths.
You can see here where it's dented
from the fight.  This pair of goblets
is priceless.  They were old Nestor's.
Look at that dove, worn smooth
from his thumb in ancient Pylos.
In this bowl Achilles ordered
that larger and stronger wine-drafts
be mixed for his friends.  And this
is the cup from which beautiful Dido
drank Bitias' health at the dinner
she gave for Trojan Aeneas."

And after you've finished admiring
the antique carvings, you're served
green wine in the prehistoric silver.

## VIII, ix

Recently, when Hylas' eyesight
was beginning to fail, Quintus,
he offered to pay you three-quarters
of what he owes you. Now
he's lost one eye and will settle
for half. Take it while you can!
A chance like this won't last
forever. If Hylas goes blind,
he'll never pay you a cent.

## VIII, x

Bassus has bought himself a cloak
for ten thousand sesterces. Purple—
the very best dyes. He's got
a real bargain.

        "A bargain?" you ask,
"at such a price?"

        Certainly,
because he'll never pay.

## VIII, xii

Why don't I marry a rich wife?
Because I won't make my wife
my master. A wife should be
submissive to her husband, Priscus.
There's no other way to give men
an equal chance with their women.

## VIII, xiv

So your fruit-trees from Cilicia
won't turn yellow and shrivel up
in the cold, or their tender branches
be nipped by too frosty a wind,
glass frames on the southern side
shut out the wind and let in
the sunlight, filtered and pure.

But I'm assigned to an attic
with a window that won't shut tight
in which Boreas himself
would be miserable. Is this
how you, cruelest of patrons,
expect an old friend to live?
If so, I'd be better protected
as a guest of one of your trees.

## VIII, xvii

I pleaded your case, Sextus,
for a fee of two thousand sesterces.
Agreed? Then why do you send me
a  thousand?

         "You never uttered
a word. It's because of you
I lost it!"

         All the more reason
for paying what you owe, Sextus.
I did your blushing for you.

## VIII, xix

Cinna wants us to think his poverty
is a pose. Actually
he's as poor as he seems to be.

## VIII, xxiii

You think I'm hard-hearted, Rusticus,
and too much in love with my belly
because I gave my cook a beating
for serving up a bad dinner.
If that isn't grounds enough
for a thrashing, what on earth
would one beat one's cook for?


## VIII, xxv

You came to see me only once
all the time I was sick, Oppianus.
If I'd had to see you oftener
I might never have survived.


## VIII, xxvii

Gaurus, whoever gives you presents
now you're old and rich is saying
(if you had the wit to perceive it)
"Hurry up, old man, and die!"


## VIII, xxix

Anybody who writes couplets
is hoping, I suppose, to please
with their brevity. Then tell me,
if brevity's so important,
why write a whole book of them?

## VIII, xxxiii

You call this a cup, Paulus—
this sliver of gold leaf
from your praetor's crown? Or is it
a layer of the gilt paint
that used to cover the stage-machine
in the amphitheater, until
the sprinklings of red saffron-water
washed it away? Or perhaps
it's a flake some enterprising slave
chipped from the leg of your day-bed
with his fingernail. It quivers
when a gnat flies by at a distance,
and the tiniest butterfly's wing
sets it in motion. The heat
from a small lamp makes it rise,
suspended in air, and a drop
of wine would dissolve it altogether.
It's like a foil which the nuts
a threadbare client at New Year's
brings with his handful of pennies
are wrapped in. The bean-flower's tendrils
grow less delicately, and lily-leaves
that wilt in the sun are coarser
in texture. There isn't a spider
that roams such a tenuous web
or a cradled silkworm that spins
such a flimsy thread. The powder
of old Fabulla's face is thicker,
and so are the bubbles on water
when it's stirred. The hairnets girls
bind up their curls with are stronger
and so is the hair-wash they use
to turn themselves into redheads.

Chicks in their shells have a skin
like this, and the crescent patches
our ladies stick on their faces
are no thinner. Why this cup
when you might have sent me a tablespoon
or a teaspoon, or if that's
asking too much, a toothpick,
Paulus—or nothing at all?

## VIII, xli

Athenagoras says he's sorry
he didn't send me the presents
he usually does at New Year's.
I don't know whether Athenagoras
is really sorry, Faustinus,
but I am.

## VIII, xliii

Fabius buries his wives,
Chrestilla her husbands, and both
wave the funeral torches over
the marriage-bed. Match the winners,
Venus! Let the same fate
await them both: a single
funeral suitable for two.

## VIII, xliv

Enjoy life, Titullus. I warn you,
it's always later than you think.
If you start in as a schoolboy,
it's already late. But you,
poor Titullus, aren't alive
even in old age. Instead
you're wearing out every doorsill
in town paying calls. You begin
every morning in a sweat, slobbered
all over with everybody's kisses,
and throughout the middle of the day
you're hurrying through the three forums
(past all the equestrian statues
and the Temple of Mars and Augustus'
huge statue) splashed with mud.
Grab and steal, scratch and save,
you can't take any of it with you.
Stuff your arrogant money-boxes
with yellow coins and fill up
a hundred pages with the debts
falling due on the Kalends. Your heir
will insist that you left him nothing.
As soon as you've been laid out
on a slab and the funeral fire,
stuffed with paper, is leaping high,
the insolent fellow will be kissing
the weeping eunuchs, and (whether
you like it or not) your son
in his grief, the very first night,
will sleep with your favorite boy.

## VIII, xlvi

Your childish beauty is equalled
by your modesty, young Cestus,
chaster than boyish Hippolytus.
Diana would let you swim with her
and give you lessons. Cybele
would rather have you beside her
than womanish Attis. You're worthy
of Ganymede's bed. But you'd never
give more than kisses to your lord
in your obstinacy. How happy
the bride will be who arouses
her gentle husband—the girl
who first makes a man of you!


## VIII, xlviii

Crispinus can't remember
who he handed his purple cloak to
while he was changing his clothes
and putting on his toga. Whoever
you are that has it, we beg you,
restore that noble ornament
to his shoulders. It isn't Crispinus
that asks you, it's the cloak.
Not everybody can wear
a purple-dyed robe. That color
requires a certain stylishness
in the wearer. If stealing's your weakness,
and a rage for other people's things,
pick out an ordinary toga.
You're more likely to get away with it.

## VIII, liii

Most beautiful of all women
who are or ever have been
and most dissolute of them all
who are or ever have been—
o how I wish, Catulla,
you'd become less beautiful
or develop a sense of shame!


## VIII, lix

You see that fellow who's contented
to get along with one eye—
with a sightless cavity gaping
underneath his shameless brow?
Don't underestimate him. No one's
a bigger thief than he is.
Autolycus's own hand
was never as quick. Remember
to keep a careful eye on him
when he's visiting. It's then
he runs wild, and with his one eye
sees enough for both. Your servants
will be worried when cups and spoons
turn up missing, and many a napkin
gets hidden in his sweaty bosom.
He knows how to lift a mantle
hanging loose on your elbow, and often
he wears two cloaks, going home.
He wouldn't hesitate to steal
an oil-lamp from a sleeping slave—
still burning, the scoundrel. If nothing
else is available, he'll practice
his trickery on your houseboy
by stealing his own sandals.

## VIII, lxi

Charinus is green with envy—
almost ready to burst. He rages.
He weeps. He's looking for branches
high enough to hang himself from.
And this time it isn't because
I'm read and recited everywhere
in the world or because my books,
tricked out with bosses and cedar oil,
are scattered abroad among the nations
Rome controls, but because, in the suburbs,
I own a little country-place
and the mules that pull my go-cart
aren't hired from a livery stable
anymore. Severus, what curses
shall I call down on his green looks?
Here's my wish: let *him* have mules
and a farm to worry about.


## VIII, lxix

You admire only the ancients,
Vacerra, and won't praise poets
unless they're dead. Forgive me,
Vacerra, I beg you. It isn't
worth dying just to make you like me.

## VIII, lxxiii

Instantius, no one's considered
a truer friend, or superior
to you in honesty and candor.
So if you'd like to give strength
and liveliness to my Muse
and are on the lookout for poems
that will live, just give me someone
to love. Your Cynthia made you
a poet, wanton Propertius.
And Gallus's inspiration
was beautiful Lycoris. Fame
came to sweet-singing Tibullus
through lovely Nemesis. And you,
erudite Catullus, were prompted
by Lesbia. Ovid's townsmen
wouldn't spurn me as a poet,
or Vergil's, if some Corinna
or Alexis were my very own.

## VIII, lxxix

All your girl friends are old hags
or ugly women, more hideous
than old hags. You take them with you
wherever you go, as companions—
dragging them along to parties
and on strolls through the porticos
and to the theater. This way
you always seem beautiful,
Fabulla, and young.

# BOOK IX

## IX, ii

You're a poor man to your friends
but not to your mistress, Lupus,
and that fellow between your thighs
is the only one without a grievance
against you. While your adulteress
is fattening herself on wheat-loaves
shaped like women's cunts, you feed
your guest on black bread. You pour out
Setine wine to warm up your mistress
and put her in the mood. I drink
the muddiest kind of poison
from a Corsican jar. You squander
your father's inheritance to pay
for her not so exclusive favors.
Your neglected friend does his plowing
in fields that don't belong to him.
Your whore is shining and glittering
in jewels from the East. Your comrade
is arrested and carted off to jail
while you're having your fun in bed.
You provide your girl with a litter
carried by eight Syrian slaves.
But your friend will be lugged, stark naked,
on a pauper's bier. Now, Cybele,
why castrate those wretched fairies?
Here's a lecher worthy of your knife.

## IX, v

You want to marry Priscus.
I don't wonder, Paula. You're wise.
But Priscus doesn't want to marry
you. He's wise, too.


## IX, vii

When you came home from Libya
I tried to say hello to you
for five days running, Afer.
All they told me was "He's busy"
or "He's asleep" when I went back
two or three times. Enough's
enough! Since you're not interested
in hellos, Afer—goodbye.


## IX, xiv

This man your table and your dinners
have made your friend—do you suppose
his heart's full of loyalty and love?
It's boar he loves, and mullet,
and sow's tits, and oysters,
not you. He'll be *my* friend
if I serve such wonderful dinners.


## IX, xix

You praise in three hundred verses
the baths of Ponticus, who gives
good dinners, Sabellus. It's dinner
you're after, not a bath.

## IX, xxv

That's a rather disconsolate look
you're watching us with, Afer,
as we glance so often at your Hyllus,
serving the wine.  But is it—
I ask you—is it a crime
to stare at a modest serving-boy?
We look at the sun, the stars,
temples and statues of the gods.
Am I supposed to turn away
my face, as if he were a Gorgon
handing me a cup and attacking
my eyes and face?  Hercules,
that roughneck, wasn't prevented
from looking at Hylas.  Mercury
was allowed to play with Ganymede.
If you don't like your guests staring
at your young serving-boys, Afer,
you better invite only blind men
like Phineus and Oedipus.

## IX, xxxii

I like a girl who's willing.
I like a girl who runs around
in a little Greek cape—who's given
herself already to my slave-boy.
I like a girl you can buy
outright for a second denarius.
I like a girl who can satisfy
three lovers at once, by herself.
The girls who are full of big talk
and out for the money—some stupid
Gascon lecher can have them.

## IX, xlviii

When you swore by everything sacred
and your own head, Garricus,
that a fourth of all your wealth
would be willed to me, I believed you.
(Who ever wants to disbelieve
what he hopes is true?) I kept
my hopes up by giving you presents
on every occasion. I sent you
a Laurentian boar of unusual
size, among other things.
You'd think it had come from Calydon
in Aetolia. You invited
everybody right away—
the senators and all the citizens—
and an overstuffed Rome is still belching
from my boar. But (who'd believe it?)
I myself wasn't even tacked on
at the bottom of your guest-list. No,
I wasn't even sent a rib
or the tail. What am I to think
about that quarter of your fortune,
Garricus, when I never saw
a fraction of my own boar?

## IX, 1

You prove my talent's a small one
on the ground that I write poems
that please with their brevity, Gaurus.
I plead guilty. But you, who tell us
in a dozen bombastic volumes
about Priam's wars—are you
a great poet? I make Brutus'
boy statuette come alive,
and other small things. But you,
great poet that you are, Gaurus,
make a giant—out of clay.

## IX, liii

I wanted to give you a present
for your birthday, Quintus. A small one.
You said no, and you're a man
who knows his own mind. Your orders
must be obeyed. Let's do something
we both want—something we'll both
like, Quintus. You give me one.

## IX, lxvi

Since you have a wife who's beautiful
and modest and still a girl,
Fabullus, why are you applying
for the rights of a father of three sons?
This thing you're humbly beseeching
of our lord and god, you yourself
will supply—if you're a man.

## IX, lxviii

Have you got a grudge against me,
you miserable schoolmaster—
a fellow hated by the boys
and girls. The crested roosters
haven't broken the night's silence
and already you're raising a rumpus
with your slappings and your angry voice.
It's as noisy as brass being beaten
on anvils whenever a blacksmith
is fitting an advocate's statue
to a metal steed. The clamor
that breaks out when the different factions
are cheering for their gladiators
in the amphitheater's milder.
We neighbors don't expect to sleep
all night undisturbed. Being waked up
once in awhile isn't serious.
But keeping us awake all night—
that's a different story. Dismiss
your pupils, and listen, loudmouth.
Will you take whatever they're paying you
to make all that racket, and keep still?


## IX, lxx

Cicero cried "O tempora!
O mores!" when Cataline
was plotting his sacrilegious crime—
when son-in-law and father-in-law
came together in terrifying wars
and the sorrowing earth was stained
with civil blood. Now *you're* crying
"O tempora!" and "O mores!"
Caecilianus. Why is it?

What's bothering you? No savagery
of the generals, no insanity
of the sword is here. We're free
to enjoy our peace and happiness
undisturbed. It isn't *our* manners
that make the times seem bad to you,
Caecilianus. It's your own.

## IX, lxxiii

Your trade was stretching old hides
with your teeth and chewing shoe-soles,
worn out and filthy with grime.
Now you own the Praenestan fields
of your dead patron (though I
think an attic's too good for you).
You get drunk on old Falernian
and break the glasses and play
naughty games with your old master's
serving-boy. *My* foolish parents
taught me useless letters. What good
were my teachers of grammar and rhetoric?
Break your silly pens, Thalia,
my Muse. Tear up your books,
if a shoe gives a shoemaker this.

## IX, lxxviii

After burying seven husbands,
Galla's married you, Picentinus.
I guess she wants to go the way
those husbands did.

## IX, lxxxi

Readers and listeners like
my books, but a certain poet
says they lack polish, Aulus.
That doesn't bother me much,
since I plan my dinners to please
the diners, not the cooks.

## IX, lxxxv

Whenever our friend Paulus
isn't feeling well, Atilius,
he goes on a diet—not
for himself but for his guests.
You must have had an attack
just now, Paulus. At any rate,
my dinner has turned up its toes.

## IX, xcii

You've no idea, Condylus,
what a master has to put up with
or the good side of being a slave,
or you wouldn't complain at such length
about being the latter. You sleep
undisturbed on your mat of rushes.
But see how Gaius lies awake
all night on his feather-bed!
Early every morning, Gaius
goes nervously to pay his greetings
to many masters. You, Condylus,
don't even say good morning to him.
"Pay what you owe me, Gaius,"
says Phoebus, and Cinnamus
says the same. No one says that
to you, Condylus. Perhaps
you're afraid of being tortured. Gaius
is stabbed in his feet and his hands
by the gout, and would rather endure
a thousand blows. You don't wake up
vomiting, Condylus, or practice
perversions. Now don't you prefer
what you are to being like Gaius,
your master, three times over?

## IX, xcviii

The vineyard harvest hasn't failed
everywhere, Ovidius.
The rainstorms have done some good.
Coranus, the wine-seller,
has filled a hundred jars—with water.

# BOOK X

## X, i

If I look like too big a book—
too long from beginning to end—
read part of me. Then I'll be
a small book. Often my pages
end with short poems. Make me
as short for yourself as you please.

## X, iv

When you read about Oedipus
and gloomy Thyestes—and Scyllas
and Medeas—what are you reading
but fairy tales? What difference
can they make for you—Hylas' rape,
or Parthenopaeus and Attis,
or Endymion sleeping? Or the boy
whose wings fell off when he was flying?
Or Hermaphroditus, who hated
the waters that loved him? Why
should such wretched pages attract you
with their useless nonsense? Read
these, of which life itself can say
"That's mine." You won't find Centaurs
or Gorgons or Harpies. My pages
tell about men. But, Mamurra,
if you'd rather not recognize
your own weaknesses or acquire
some insight into your own nature,
read Callimachus's *Origins*.

## X, viii

Paula wants to marry me,
but I don't want to marry Paula.
She's old. I might be willing
if she were even older.

## X, xiii

Your effeminate slaves are carried
in a travelling-coach and followed
by a Libyan rider who sweats
along in the dust. Your bathing-pools—
more than one—are ringed with couches,
well-upholstered, and your sea-bath
is tinted with expensive perfumes.
Your crystal goblets are filled
to the brim with Setine wine
and Venus herself never slept
in a softer feather-bed. Still,
you spend every night on the doorstep
of a stuck-up bitch, and her door,
deaf and dumb, is soaked with your tears.
So sad! And the sighs never stop,
welling from your troubled heart.
Shall I tell you what's the matter,
Cotta? You've got it too good.

## X, xxix

The dish you used to send me
at the Saturnalia, you send
to your mistress now, Sextilianus.
And the money for a birthday toga
you'd give me at the March Kalends
goes to buy the lady a green gown.
You're getting your girls for nothing
these days, Sextilianus.
My presents are paying for your sex-life.

## X, xxxvii

Most conscientious supporter
of justice and equitable laws,
you dominate the Latin forum
with your honest speeches, Maternus.
If there's anything an old friend
and fellow townsman can do for you
in the region of the Spanish Ocean—

Or do you imagine it's better
to catch a few ugly frogs
and minnows here by the shore
of Laurentium, than to throw back
to its place among the rocks a mullet
you've caught, because it might weigh
less than three pounds? Or to dine
on insipid mussels and shell-fish
set out at the head of the table
as a special treat, instead of oysters
as good as the ones at Baiae
which slaves themselves gobble down
with their masters' permission? Here
your shouts drive a stinking fox
into your nets, and the worthless

quarry bites your hounds.  There
a net just hauled out of the sea
that's alive with fish—still dripping—
will catch me a mess of rabbits.
Look, while I'm talking, your fisherman
is bringing home an empty creel,
and your huntsman will show up, delighted
at having caught himself a badger!
Your whole sea-side dinner's provided
from the food-market in town.

If there's anything I can do for you
in the region of the Spanish Ocean—


### X, xl

Since everybody was saying
my Polla's been going around
secretly with a fairy,
I broke in upon them, Lupus.
That fellow's no fairy.


### X, xlv

If my little book contains anything
gentle and pleasant, or my poems
praise anybody out of kindness,
you call it insipid and prefer
gnawing a rib, though I offer you
the loin of a Laurentian boar.
If you've a taste for vinegar,
drink Vatican. My wine-jar
will never suit your stomach.

## X, xlvii

These things, dearest Julius Martial,
make life more pleasant: money
inherited, not earned;
fields that bring in a good harvest
and a kitchen fire that never
goes out; no lawsuits, and seldom
the necessity for wearing a toga;
a quiet mind; a strong body
and a healthy one; candor
accompanied by tact; good friends;
easy-going guests; a table
plainly furnished; sober nights
free from worry; a marriage-bed
not puritanical but chaste;
sleep which makes the dark hours
brief. Enjoy what you are.
Don't long for change. Neither dread
your dying day nor yearn for it.

## X, xlviii

Now the crowds in Isis' temple
are announcing the eighth hour
to the heifer-goddess from Egypt,
and the guards are being relieved
and sent back to their quarters.
At this hour the warm baths,
steaming hot the hour before
and fiery as Nero's in the sixth,
are becoming more moderate.

Stella, Nepos, Canius,
Cerialis, Flaccus, won't you come
to dinner? My C-shaped couch
holds seven. There are six of us.

We'll add Lupus.  My caretaker's
wife brought me mallows, to relieve
our stomachs, and all the good things
that grow in the kitchen-garden.
Fat lettuce-heads are among them,
and little green onions, and mint
to make you belch, and herbs
to stimulate your potency.

We'll have sea-lizard, served with rue
and garnished with egg-slices,
and sow's tits marinated
in tuna-fish sauce.  So much
for appetizers.  Your supper
will be served in a single dish:
a kid rescued from the jaws
of a savage wolf, and meat-balls
that require no carving-knife,
and beans, the workingman's food,
and tender cabbage-sprouts.  Add to these
a chicken and a leg of pork
that's already outlasted three dinners.

When you've eaten enough, I'll give you
ripe apples and Nomentan wine,
without dregs, that was one year old
in Frontinus' second consulship.
To finish things off, we'll have jokes
without malice and the kind of freedom
you won't be ashamed of next morning,
and nothing you'll wish you hadn't said.
We can argue about the races
in the Colosseum.  My wine-cups
won't hail anybody into court.

### X, xlix

While you drink from amethyst cups
and drown yourself in black Opimian,
Cotta, you give me green Sabine
and ask "Would you like your wine
in a gold cup?" Who wants
to drink leaden wine from gold?

### X, lix

If a poem takes up a whole page,
you skip it and prefer the shorter,
not the better epigrams. A dinner,
furnished with expensive things
from every market, has been placed
before you, but you only choose
the delicacies. I don't like
too finicky a reader. I'd rather
have the kind who insists on bread.

### X, lxii

Have mercy on your little flock,
schoolmaster, and curly-haired boys
will crowd around you and listen,
and the gentle group around your desk
will like you. You'll be as popular
as the teacher of arithmetic
or short-hand. The hot days
blaze under fiery Leo,
and burning July is ripening
the parched grain. Let the Scythian
whip, with its bristling thongs
(with which Marsyas of Celaenae
was flayed), and the terrifying ferule
(the pedagogue's scepter) have a rest.
Let them sleep till the Ides of October.

If boys can stay out of trouble
all summer, they're learning enough.

## X, lxv

You call yourself a fellow-townsman
of the Corinthians (and no one
denies it, Charmenion).
So why should you call me brother—
a Celt and an Iberian
and a citizen of Tagus?
Do we look alike? You stroll around
looking glossy with your wavy hair.
Mine's unruly in the Spanish fashion.
You shave all over, every day.
My legs and cheeks are hairy.
You speak with a lady-like voice
and a lisp. My farting's louder
than that. A dove isn't less
like an eagle, or a timid doe
like a raging lion. You'd better
quit calling me brother, Charmenion,
or I'll start calling you sister.

## X, lxvii

She's Deucalion's daughter and Nestor's
step-mother, and when Niobe
saw her as a girl was already
a crone. Ancient Laertes
called her his grandmother,
Priam his nurse, and Thyestes
his mother-in-law. Plotia,
now she's outlived all the crows,
is laid in the tomb at last,
beside bald Melanthion—
still itching with lust.

## X, lxx

Since I scarcely manage to publish
one book in an entire year,
you charge me with laziness, Potitus,
my learned friend.  You'd be fairer
if you wondered how I publish one,
when whole days slip away from me
so much of the time.  I go
before daylight to call on friends
who never return the compliment,
and offer my congratulations
to others.  No one offers them
to me, Potitus.  Sometimes
I go to the temple of Diana
the Light-Bearer to put my seal
on a document with my signet-ring.
Sometimes it's the first hour,
sometimes the fifth that snatches me
away.  Sometimes a consul
or a praetor with his crowd
of followers detains me.
And often I listen to a poet
reciting all day.  You can't
risk saying "no" to the lawyers
and grammarians and professors
of rhetoric when they make requests.
At the end of the tenth hour,
tired out, I head for the baths
and my dole of a hundred quadrantes,
Potitus.  When is there time
for a book to get itself written?

## X, lxxvi

Fortuna, do you think it's fair?
Here's a citizen, not of Syria
or Parthia (he's not a knight
who got his start in a slave-market
of Cappadocia), but home-born
of the people of Remus and Numa—
a good-natured fellow, honest,
well-behaved and friendly and learned
in either tongue. His only fault,
a large one, is that he's a poet.
It's Maevius, who's shivering
in a gray hood while Incitatus,
the mule-driver, shines in scarlet.

## X, lxxix

Torquatus owns a huge villa
four miles from town. Otacilius
bought a half-acre of land
four miles out. Torquatus constructed
warm baths, gleaming with marble
of many colors. Otacilius
built a fish-pond. Torquatus planted
a laurel-grove on his property.
Otacilius scattered handfuls
of chestnuts. Torquatus was appointed
consul. Otacilius served
as councilman for his neighborhood
and considered that honor made him
just as good a man. In the fable
the huge ox made the little frog
burst himself. I'm afraid Torquatus
will do the same for Otacilius.

## X, lxxx

Eros weeps whenever he comes across
veined alabaster cups or citrus-wood
or slave-boys handsomer than usual.
He sighs from the bottom of his heart
because, poor fellow, he can't buy
every elegant shop in the Septa
and carry it home. How many
of us are like Eros? We laugh
at his tears, without sympathy—
and weep in our own hearts.

## X, lxxxiv

Are you wondering why Afer
doesn't go to bed, Caedicianus?
Just look at the woman he's dining with.

## X, lxxxvi

No man ever loved a new mistress
as passionately as Laurus
loved playing ball. In his prime
he was a first-class player,
but now he's given up the game
he's a first-class good-for-nothing.

## X, xci

All Almo's servants are eunuchs,
and he himself is impotent.
And still he complains because Polla,
his wife, bears him no children.

## X, xcvi

Avitus, you often ask me
why I talk so much about people
far away, although I've grown old
in Rome, and why I'm homesick
for the gold-bearing Tagus and the Salo
of my native land and remember
a thriving farm's muddy fields.
I love that country where small things
make me happy, and a little money
lets me live luxuriously.
Here you must support the land.
There it's the land supports you.
Here your hearth barely loses its chill
from an unwilling fire. There
it's glowing with a mighty blaze.
Here hunger's expensive and the shops
can bankrupt you. There your table's
loaded with its own country fare.
I wear out four or more togas
in a summer here. One lasts me
four years out there. Why court
the great ones, Avitus, when there's
a place to provide you with everything
a patron fails to provide?

## X, xcvii

When the funeral pyre was being laid,
loosely, with papyruses for kindling.
When his weeping wife was buying
cinnamon and myrrh.  When the grave
and the bier and the undertaker
were ready, Numa put me down
in his will—and got well again.

## X, cii

You ask me how Philinus,
who's impotent, can be a father.
Ask Gaditanus, Avitus.
He never writes, but he's a poet.

# BOOK XI

## XI, i

Silly book, where are you going
dressed up in your holiday purple?
To see Parthenius, perhaps?
No doubt. Well, go and come back
unopened. He never reads anything
but petitions, and hasn't the leisure
for poetry, or he'd find the time
for poems of his own. You're lucky
if less important people read you.
Head for Quirinus' portico
nearby. You won't find crowds
with less on their minds at Pompey's
or Europa's or the Argonauts'.
You'll find two or three fellows there
who might look into my trifles,
fit only for the worms—but never
till the betting and the gossiping
about Scorpus and Incitatus
and the chariot races are over.

## XI, vii

One thing's certain, Paula. Whenever
you want to go meet a lover
somewhere, you can't tell that idiot,
your husband, "Caesar ordered me
to come to his villa in Alba
this morning" or "Caesar wants me
to come to Circeii." Such tricks
won't work anymore. Under Neva,
our prince, you can be a Penelope,
except that that old itch of yours
and life-long habits prevent you.
Poor lady, what will you do?
Pretend that one of your girl-friends
is under the weather? Your husband
will stick beside you like a leech
and go with you every time you visit
your brother or your mother and father.
What fraud will your ingenuity
think up next? Another adulteress
might insist she's hysterical
and wants to go sit in the baths
of Senuessa. How much better
you do it, Paula. Whenever
you're having an affair, you'd rather
just tell your husband all about it.

## XI, xv

I've written things that Cato's wife
might read—or the most puritanical
of Sabine ladies.  But I want
this little book to make you laugh,
from the first page to the last one,
and be the naughtiest of all.
Let it soak itself in wine
and sprinkle itself, unashamed,
with elegant perfumes.  Let it play
with the boys, make love to the girls,
and speak without circumlocution
of that thing from which we are born,
the father of us all, which holy
Numa called *mentula*.  Don't forget,
Apollinaris, these are poems
for the Saturnalia.  This book
doesn't reflect my own morals.

## XI, xviii

You gave me a farm in the suburbs,
Lupus, but I've got a bigger one
in my window-box.  Can you call
this a farm, where a single rue-plant
makes a grove for Diana, and the wing
of a loudmouthed cicada would cover it,
or an ant eat it up in one day?
The unopened petal of a rose
would make a roof for it, and grass
is as hard to find as the pepper-leaves
Cosmus grinds up in his perfumes.
A cucumber couldn't lie straight in it,
and a snake couldn't curl itself up
within its boundaries.  Its garden

won't support a lone caterpillar,
and a gnat would starve itself to death
feeding on the single willow-tree.
A mole does my ditching and plowing.
There's not enough room for a mushroom
to grow, or a fig to split open,
or a violet to open up its flower.
A mouse is laying waste my borders
and is dreaded by their proprietor
like the Calydonian boar.
My entire crop is snatched away
by a flying swallow in its claws,
to be stowed in its nest, and Priapus
can't half find room to stand in it,
even without his famous sickle
and his frontispiece. My harvest,
when it's reaped, will hardly fill a snail-shell,
and we'll store the new wine in a nut
sealed with pitch. You've got it wrong,
Lupus, but only by a letter
or two. When you gave me land,
I'd rather you'd given me some lunch.

## XI, xxiv

While I'm busy providing an escort
to bring you home—and listening
to your endless chatter, and praising
everything you say or do—
how many poems, Labullus,
might have been born? It's wrong,
don't you agree, if a thing
Rome reads, and strangers ask for,
and businessmen don't make fun of,
and senators memorize, and lawyers
praise, and poets pull to pieces,
is lost because of you? Is it fair,
Labullus? Is this what anyone
should have to endure: that the number
of my books should be less so the number
of your hangers-on will be more?
It's been almost thirty days now
that I've hardly completed a page.
That's what happens whenever a poet
won't settle for a dinner at home!

## XI, xxxi

He's a regular Atreus of gourds—
Caecilius.  He cuts and chops
them into a thousand small pieces
as though they were Thyestes' sons.
You'll eat them the very first thing,
as canapés, and he brings them
in with the first and second courses
and serves them up to you again
with the third.  He makes dessert of them
later on.  He gets his confectioner
to bake insipid little cakes from them
and candies in all sorts of shapes
and dates like the ones you're familiar with
in the theaters.  His cook
makes them up into various messes
(you think you're being served lentils
and beans).  He imitates mushrooms
and puddings and fish-tails and even
little fish.  His storekeeper
exercises his skill on them,
wrapping up all the different flavors
in rue-leaves.  He fills every platter
and salad-dish and little saucer
and dinner-plate with such things.
Caecilius calls this stylish
and supposes he's being elegant
with all those dishes for a penny.

## XI, xxxix

You rocked my cradle, Charidemus,
and looked after me as a boy,
and went with me everywhere I'd go.
Now the barber's cloth turns black
with my wiskers, and my girl complains
that my lips scratch when I kiss her,
but to you I'm not a day older.
You bully my housekeeper
and the man who keeps my accounts.
The whole place trembles whenever
you're around. You won't allow me
to be frivolous or flirt with girls.
You don't want me to do anything,
but you want to be free to do anything
yourself. You bawl me out.
You spy on me. You grumble
and sigh and lose your temper
and barely hold back from thrashing me.
If I dress up in a purple robe
or put grease on my hair, you shout
"Your father never did a thing
like that!" You count my wine-cups
and frown, as though they'd been filled
from a jar in your own cellar.
Enough of this! I can't stand
a family retainer who behaves
like Cato. I'm a man now.
My mistress will tell you so.

## XI, 1

You never pass up the chance
to get something out of me, Phyllis,
because I'm so crazy about you.
You're mighty clever at taking me
for all I've got.  One minute
your maid's all tears, and false ones,
because a mirror has been lost
or a ring has dropped from your finger,
or a stone from your ear.  The next
some silks that somebody's stolen
are turned to profit.  Another time
I'm confronted with an ointment box
gone dry.  Now you're after me
for a cobwebby jar of old Falernian,
so some chattering conjure-woman
will exorcise your dreams.  And now
I'm persuaded to buy a huge bass
or a two-pound mullet, because
some rich lady-friend's invited
herself to dinner at your place.
Have some shame, and a little respect
for honesty and fairness, Phyllis.
I never refuse you anything,
Phyllis.  Don't you refuse me.

## XI, lii

You'll have a nice dinner at my house,
Julius Cerialis. Come,
if you haven't a better invitation
somewhere else. Try to get here
at the eighth hour. We'll bathe
together. The baths of Stephanus
are nearby, you know. To start with
you'll have lettuce, to relax the bowels,
and green onion shoots. And pickled
tuna-fish aplenty and a small
sea-lizard, garnished with eggs
and wrapped in rue-leaves. We'll have
more eggs, baked slowly in charcoal,
and a smoked Valebran cheese.
And olives, touched by the frosts
at Picenum. That will be enough
for appetizers. Are you curious
about the rest? I'll tell lies
to make you come: fish and mussels,
and sow's tits, and fat birds
from the poultry-yard and the marshes
such as Stella himself doesn't serve
except on special occasions.
I'll promise you another thing:
I won't recite anything, even
if you yourself read your *Giants*
straight through again, or your *Pastorals,*
next best to immortal Vergil.

## XI, lx

Who's better in bed, you ask—
Phlogis or Chione? Chione's
more beautiful, but Phlogis
has an itch. The kind of an itch
that might restore Priam's potency
and keep old Nestor from feeling
his age. The kind of an itch
every man would like his own mistress
to have. One that can't be cured
by a woman doctor, but only
by a male one. But Chione
doesn't feel anything. She never
says a word to help things along.
You'd think she was somewhere else
or made of marble. You gods,
if it were suitable to make
such a large request of you, and you
were willing to grant such a precious
boon, you'd arrange things so Phlogis
had the kind of body Chione has
and Chione had Phlogis's itch!

## XI, lxii

Lesbia swears she never does it
for free. That's true. Whenever
she wants it, she pays for it herself.

## XI, lxvi

You're a spy and a blackmailer,
a forger, a pimp, a pervert,
and a trainer of gladiators,
Vacerra. I can't understand
why you aren't rich.

## XI, lxxix

Because I didn't reach your place
at the first milestone before
the tenth hour, I'm accused
of tardiness and laziness.
It isn't the road's fault.
It isn't mine, Paetus.
It's yours, for sending me
those mules of yours.

## XI, lxxxvii

You used to be rich. But then
you ran after young men. No woman
meant anything to you in those days.
Now you chase old hags. It's amazing
what poverty can do, Charidemus.
It's made a ladies' man of you.

## XI, xciii

A fire has destroyed the household
of Theodorus, the bard.
Does that make you happy, Muses,
and you, Apollo? For shame!
What a crime and scandal of the gods
house and master didn't burn together.

## XI, xcvii

I can do it four times in one night,
but damn it, I couldn't do it once
in four years with you, Telesilla!

## XI, xcviii

It's impossible to get away
from these kissers, Flaccus. They follow you,
and stop you on the streets, and run after you,
and go out of their way to meet you—
from this side and that, any time,
anywhere. No malignant ulcers
or running sores or skin disease
or filthy scabs (and no lips
smeared with greasy salve, or an icicle
hanging down from a frozen nose)
will save you. Whether you're hot
or cold, or saving your kisses
for your wedding-night, they'll kiss you.
Hiding your head in a cowl
won't help, and neither will a litter
with its roof and curtains, or even
a sedan chair, closed up tight.
The kisser will work his way in
through the tiniest crack. Not even
the consul's office, or the tribune's,
or the praetor's six attendants
with their fasces, or the proud rod
of his shouting lictor can drive
the kisser away. You could sit
in a magistrate's seat, or deliver
the nation's laws from a curule's chair.
The kisser would be climbing up
on both sides of you. He'll kiss you

when you're feverish or in tears.
He'll give you a kiss when you're yawning
or when you're swimming, and even
when you're going to the toilet. There's only
one cure for this plague. Make friends
with anyone you don't want to kiss you.


## XI, cvii

You send my book back unrolled
to the very horns, Septicianus,
as though you'd read it straight through.
You say you've read every word of it?
I believe you. I'm sure of it. I'm glad.
It's the truth. I've read through your books—
all five of them—the same way.

# Preface to Book XII

## Valerius Martial Sends Greetings
## to His Friend Priscus

I know I should offer some apology for three years of
stubborn laziness. But no such explanation would exonerate
me, even if I were still caught up in all that busyness of city
folks by means of which, I'm afraid, we more easily succeed
in making nuisances of ourselves than in being useful to our
patrons. How much less would it do so here in my provincial
solitude, where, unless I devote myself wholeheartedly to
poetry, I've no reason for having left Rome and no pleasure
in my retirement! Listen to my reasons, then:

First, and most important, I miss the audience of fellow-
citizens I'd grown accustomed to, and feel as though I'm
pleading my case in a foreign court. For whatever was pleasing in my little books was inspired by my listeners and readers.
That discrimination of taste; those occasions that moved me
to write; the libraries, the theaters, the public gathering-places
where we acquire experience without realizing it, while we're
enjoying ourselves—all those things, in short, which I threw
away like a spoiled child—I regret now, like a person who's
lost everything.

Add to this the backbiting of my fellow-townsmen, envy
instead of criticism, and one or two real enemies—that's a lot
in this small place—and it's hard, under the circumstances, to
put up with, from day to day. You needn't be surprised, then,
if I've thrown aside in disgust the work I used to undertake
with enthusiasm.

But so as not to deny you anything you might inquire for
on coming back to the City (and I'd hardly be fulfilling my
debt of thanks by undertaking something that came easily),
I've set myself as a task what I used to indulge in for pleasure.

I've devoted a very few days to writing, so that I might greet your ears—the friendliest ones I know—with the kind of welcome they deserve.

I hope you won't think it too much trouble to judge this work and criticize it. I wouldn't consider it safe in anyone's hands but yours. And although I know how very difficult it will be for you to evaluate my trifles objectively, it's up to you to decide whether they will do—to keep me from sending off to Rome a book not just written in the provinces but provincial through and through.

## XII, vii

If Ligeia figured her age
by the number of hairs on her head,
it would make her three years old.

## XII, x

Africanus has a hundred million
but has his hooks out for more.
Lady Luck's too generous with some
but never gives anyone enough.

## XII, xii

When you've been drinking all night
you'll promise anything, Pollis.
Next day you take it all back.
Why don't you drink in the daytime?

## XII, xvii

You ask why your fever hangs on
so long, Laetinus, and keeps you
complaining?  It rides in your litter
and goes to the baths with you
and dines on mushrooms and oysters
and sows' tits and boar with you.
It often gets drunk on Setine
or Falernian and never touches
Caecuban wine unless it's filtered
through snow.  It reclines at the table
crowned with roses and balsam wreaths
and sleeps in a purple feather-bed.
Living on the fat of the land
with you, and everything so nice,
do you think it will pull up stakes
and go live with Dama, the slave?

## XII, xxv

Whenever I ask you for money
without security, you say
"I haven't a cent."  On the other hand,
you've plenty when my little farm
underwrites the loan for me.
Am I to think, Telesinus,
you don't trust me, your old friend,
as much as my cabbages and trees?

Look, Carus the informer
has entered a charge against you!
My little farm will testify
in court for you.

   You're looking
for a friend to accompany you
in exile?  My farm will go.

## XII, xxvi

Since you, a senator, set foot
on six hundred doorsills every morning,
you consider me a lazy fellow
because I'm not scouring the city
from the crack of dawn and bringing home,
wearily, a thousand kisses.
You do this to get yourself appointed
consul or ruler of the tribes
in Numidia or Cappadocia.
But I, whom you force to break off
my sleep in the middle and go tramping
through the early morning mud—what's in it
for me? When my foot's gaping
from a broken shoe and the rain's
coming down in sudden heavy gusts
and the servant who's carrying my cloak
won't come when I shout for him, a slave
sidles up to my half-frozen ear
to say "Laetorius invites you
to dinner at his house." At twenty
sesterces a head? Not I.
I'd rather starve than be given
a dinner while you get a province
for your reward. Are we expected
to do the same work, for different pay?

## XII, xxix

When it comes to napkins, Hermogenes
is as big a thief as Massa was
about money. I'll swear to it, Ponticus.
You can hold the fellow by one hand
and keep your eye on the other—
he'll manage to pilfer a napkin
somehow, the way they say stags
suck up clammy snakes from their holes
with their breath, or the way Iris
draws up the water that falls
afterward, from the sky.
Just the other day, when handkerchiefs
were waved as a signal to spare
Myrinus, the wounded gladiator,
Hermongenes swiped four of them.
When the praetor was ready to drop
his white handkerchief at the start
of a horserace, our friend Hermogenes
stole *that*. If no one brings napkins
to dinner for fear of thievery,
Hermogenes steals the tablecloth,
and if there isn't one of these,
Hermogenes won't hesitate to steal
the slip-covers from the couches
or the wrappings from the table legs.
Suppose the arena is simmering
under a blistering sun.
They'll roll up the awnings, all the same,
when Hermogenes shows up.
Sailors haul in their sails,
in a panic, when Hermogenes
enters the harbor. And priests
with their shaven heads among the crowds

of timbrel-shakers, run away
in their linen robes when Hermogenes
takes his place among the worshippers.
Hermogenes has never brought
a napkin to dinner, but he always
carries one away with him.

## XII, xxxi

This stand of trees. These springs.
The pleached shade of arching trees.
The little canal of running water.
The grassfields. The rosebeds
unsurpassed even at Paestum
with its double blossoming season.
The green herb garden which never
freezes, even in mid-winter.
My own tame eel that swims
in the covered pond. The white dovehouse
with its birds as white as itself.
All these are gifts from my lady.
All these Marcella gave me,
come home after thirty-four years—
this house, this little kingdom.
If Nausicaa should offer me
her father's gardens, I could say
to Alcinous "I'll keep my own."

## XII, xxxii

You disgrace the city of Rome
on moving day, Vacerra.
I've seen your traps. At least
I've seen what's left of them
after the rest have been seized
by the landlord for two years' rent
you didn't pay. They were lugged
by your wife with her seven red curls
and your white-haired mother and that
huge sister of yours. I thought
they were Furies, come from the blackness
of Hell: the ladies marching
up in front, and you, all shrivelled
with cold and hunger and paler
than bleached-out boxwood, trailing
along like a beggar behind.
It looked just like moving day
on Paupers' Hill: a day-bed
with three legs, a table with two
jogged along, and tumbled together
were a lantern, a cheap wooden bowl,
and a broken chamberpot, pissing
through a hole in its side. The neck
of a winejar was lying underneath
a charcoal stove, green with age.
And hidden inside the load
were salt-fish or half-rotten herrings.
The unholy stink of the storage-pot
gave them away—such a stink
as a fish-pond could hardly come up with.
And the usual hunk of stale cheese
from Toulouse, and a four-year old wreath
of mintleaves, blackened with smoke,

and old strings that used to hold garlic
and onions, and your mother's pot
of putrid resin—the kind
whores use to keep the hair down.
Why all this scrounging for houses
and dodging of landlords, Vacerra,
when you could be living for free?
That parade of junk you were carrying
would look right at home in Beggarstown,
underneath the city bridge.


## XII, xxxiv

If my memory's correct,
Julius Martial, we've been friends
for thirty-four years. They were years
of good and bad mixed, but with more
of pleasantness than otherwise.
And if all the pebbles of those days
were sorted into separate piles
of two colors, on this side and that,
the whites would outnumber the blacks.
If you want to escape unpleasantness
altogether and keep your guard up
against every trouble that eats
a man's heart, don't let yourself become
too much of a friend to anyone.
You'll enjoy life less that way
and have fewer things to regret.

## XII, xxxv

Just as if we had no secrets
from one another, Callistratus,
you're in the habit of telling me,
often, of your love-affairs.
Still, you're not as frank as you'd like me
to think, Callistratus. Anyone
who talks so freely of such things
is covering up something worse.

## XII, xxxvi

Four pounds of plated silver,
or two, given to a friend,
or a bob-tailed cloak or a toga
so thin it won't keep out the cold,
or now and then a few coins
to jingle in the hand (enough
to stretch for a couple of months,
perhaps)—just because no one
but you gives even this much,
Labullus, that doesn't make you
a model patron, believe me.
What does it make you? To tell
the truth, it makes you the best
of a rather sorry lot. Just give me
the Pisos and Senecas again,
the Mummiuses and Crispuses
of the old days. Immediately,
you'd be the worst of a good lot.
If you're looking for fame as a racer,
beat Tigris, beat Passarinus—
horses that can run. There's no glory
in winning a race against donkeys.

## XII, xxxviii

That fellow who goes promenading
day and night in women's sedan chairs—
the whole city's talking about him
with his well-groomed hair, dark and oily,
his purple robes, his bedroom eyes,
his depilated legs and chest.
He's the one who hangs around your wife
all the time, as if he were a lover.
But don't let it worry you, Candidus.
He's impotent.

## XII, xl

You tell lies; I believe you.
You read your miserable poems;
I praise them.
        You sing; I sing.
You drink, Pontilianus;
I drink too.
        You fart; I pretend
not to hear.
        You're in the mood for chess;
I lose.
        There's one thing you do
when I'm not around; I keep my mouth shut.
Yet you promise me nothing at all.
You say "When I die, I'll treat you
right."
        There's nothing I'm after,
but won't you hurry up and die.

## XII, xlviii

If you'll serve your mushrooms and boar
like ordinary fare, I'll come.
But if you think I'm getting rich
and hope to be mentioned in my will
as payment for half a dozen oysters,
nothing doing! I'll grant your dinner
is sumptuous—sumptuissimus.
But what will it amount to tomorrow,
or today, even, or an hour
from now—nothing a poor sponge
on a dirty stick won't soak up,
or any stray dog, or a urinal
beside the road. The end-product
of mullets and hares and sows' tits
is this: a greenish complexion
and feet tortured with the gout!
Not even the Emperor's revels
or the high priests' banquets for Jupiter
and the other gods would be worth it
for me. And a god himself
might make me obliged to him for nectar:
it would all turn to vinegar
and the disappointing tastelessness
of a jug of Vatican. Find
others, as master of the feast,
whom the princely magnificence
of your table will attract. As for me,
let a friend invite me to supper
of the pick-up kind. The dinner
I like is the one I can return.

## XII, li

Why should you be surprised,
Aulus, that our friend Fabullinus
is so often taken in. A good man's
always something of a sucker.

## XII, lvi

Ten times a year, Polycharmus,
you get sick—or oftener.
You seem to be able to stand it,
but it's hard on us, your friends.
Every time you get well, we're expected
to furnish gifts for the occasion.
Have some shame! This time, Polycharmus,
get it over with, once and for all.

## XII, lvii

You wonder why I retreat
so often to my barren acres
and shabby farmhouse at Nomentum?
It's because there's no place in the city
for a poor man to get a little peace
and a chance to think, Sparsus.
In the morning it's the schoolmasters
who make life impossible,
and the bakers, even before daylight,
and the coppersmiths' hammering
all day long. The money-changer
over there keeps jingling his pile
of short-weight coins from Nero's day,
having nothing to do. Over here
a goldbeater's beating out gold dust
from Spain with his glinting hammer
on a worn stone anvil. Worshippers
of goddess Bellona, in their frenzy,
never stop shouting, and neither
does the loud-mouthed shipwrecked sailor
crying pity for his bandaged leg,
or the Jewish boy trained by his mother
to beg, or the bleary-eyed huckster
of sulphur-matches. Somebody
with patience enough to keep track
of all the interruptions that shatter
our blessed sleep may be able
to tell you how many brass kitchen-pots
are banged together by the citizens
whenever the moon, in eclipse,
is being assaulted, they suppose,
by witches with their magic-wheels.
You, Sparsus, know nothing of all this

and you can't be expected to know,
off there in your elegant mansion
whose ground-floor looks down on hill-tops—
a country estate inside the city,
with vineyards the hills of Falernus
can't outproduce, here in Rome,
and broad boulevards for carriage-riding
inside your own boundaries, and sleep
undisturbed, and quietness
unbroken by voices, and daylight
only when you choose to let it in.
With me, the laughter of the crowds
going by in the street wakes me up
and all of Rome seems to be gathered
by my bedside. When the whole thing's
too much for me and I'm dying
for sleep, I escape to my farm.

## XII, lxi

You're afraid I'll satirize you
in a poem—some lively epigram—
and you'd like to think yourself worthy
of such a threat, Ligurra.
But your worrying and hoping
are useless. African lions
rage at bulls. They leave butterflies
alone. If you're so anxious
to get yourself into a poem,
go hunt up some drunken poet
sprawling in his dirty cellar
who scrawls his verses with fragments
of charcoal or broken chalk
on shithouse walls. Your forehead
won't be dignified with my brand.

## XII, lxiii

Cordova, richer than Venafrum
in olive oil no way inferior
in quality to that of Istria—
whose sheep are finer than the snowy
flocks of Galaesus—their fleeces
naturally golden, untainted
with tints of blood or sea-shell dyes—
won't you order that poet of yours,
please, to have some decency
and quit plagiarizing my poems
without payment or acknowledgment.
I could stand it if a good poet
did this—a poet I can give
the same treatment back again.
But a bachelor can seduce
other men's wives with impunity.
And you can't get an eye for an eye
from a blind man.  And there's nothing
more frustrating than a thief
with nothing to steal.  No one's safer
from reprisals than a pilfering poet
whose own stuff's not worth taking.

## XII, lxv

After lovely Phyllis had given herself
generously, in every way
all night long, and I was considering
next morning what sort of present
I ought to give her—a pound
of face-cream from Cosmus or Niceros,
the perfumers, or a heavy skein
of Baetic wool, or a dozen
of Caesar's yellow coins—Phyllis,
wrapping her arms around my neck
and coaxing me with a kiss
as lingering as a mating dove
might give, began teasing me
to buy her a jug of wine!

## XII, lxviii

It's early-bird callers like you
that made me leave Rome. If you had
any sense, you'd be haunting the courtyards
of ambitious men. I'm not
a pleader, and I have no taste
for contentious lawsuits. Rather,
I'm a lazy fellow, growing old,
who likes to write poems. Rest
and sleep are what I crave—the things
Rome's mighty city denied me.
But I'll go back if I can't
find them even here in Spain.

## XII, lxx

In the old days, when his towels
were carried by a bow-legged boy,
and a one-eyed hag kept watch
on his bob-tailed toga, and his drop
of oil was squeezed out for him
by a ruptured bath-attendant,
Aper was a bitter, outspoken
critic of anyone who drank.
He used to demand that the cups
which a fellow-bather was drinking from
be smashed, and the good Falernian
poured out on the ground. But now,
since he got three hundred thousand
sesterces in his uncle's will,
he can't even get home sober
from the baths. It's remarkable
what a difference a few carved wine-cups
and five long-haired slaves can make.
In the old days, when he was poor,
he never even got thirsty!

## XII, lxxii

Now you've bought yourself a few acres
of farmland, lost among the tombs
that line the roads from Rome, Pannychus—
and a tumble-down shack with a roof
propped up with timbers—you've quit
the fertile fields of city lawsuits
where you earned a steady living,
however modest, in your threadbare
lawyers' gown. You used to sell
wheat, millet, barley, and beans
as a man of affairs. You *buy* them
now that you've turned farmer.

## XII, lxxvi

Twenty cents for a jug of wine.
A peck of wheat sells for four.
The farmers are all drunk,
and eat too much, and are broke.

## XII, lxxx

So as not to give credit to those
who deserve it, Callistratus praises
everyone. No one's very good
if you don't think anybody's bad.

## XII, xciv

I was writing an epic; you
began writing one too. I stopped,
so my verses wouldn't be competing
with yours.

        Thalia, my muse,
switched to tragedy; you put on
the trailing tragic mantle too.

I plucked the strings of the lyre
Horace played upon; you stole
my pick before I'd got used to it
in your eagerness for fame.

I try satire; immediately
you've got to be a Lucilius.
I play with light elegies;
you play around with them too.

Can I find a literary genre
more minor still? I begin
composing epigrams; here too
you're out to steal my reputation.

Pick out something you don't want
to write (it isn't very modest
to want to write everything yourself),
and once you find me such a thing,
keep your dirty hands off it, Tucca!

Martial often described volumes of his poetry as "wrapped up in a soft purple cover with your title glowing magnificently in scarlet" (III,ii). These colors were used on the jacket by book designer Moroni J. St. John, who incorporated sketches by Iola J. Mills. Jackets were printed by Owen Litho Service, Spencer, Indiana. Caslon Old Style type was used for the text, printed on 60 lb. Warren's Olde Style paper. C. E. Pauley and Co., Indianapolis, Indiana, was the printer and the Modern Binding Corporation of Portland, Indiana, was the binder. Editorial and production work were supervised by Eleanor Crandall and Diane Dubiel.

# BREAKING INTO PRINT

*Books by Edward Weeks*

THE OPEN HEART
IN FRIENDLY CANDOR
THIS TRADE OF WRITING
GREAT SHORT NOVELS, an anthology
JUBILEE, the *Atlantic* anthology
  (ed. with Emily Flint)

# BREAKING

## ❧ INTO PRINT

### An Editor's Advice on Writing

By EDWARD WEEKS

EDITOR, *The Atlantic Monthly*

THE WRITER, INC. · PUBLISHERS · BOSTON

To Sylvia *and* Abe Burack
*for the help they have given others*

# ✳ FOREWORD

In the mid 1930's when I had been editing for less than a decade, I published some observations and conclusions addressed to the beginning writer and entitled This Trade of Writing. It was a young book with much hope and a little vinegar; it held out both encouragement and practical advice which I felt might be helpful during those depression years, and it added to my self-confidence by passing through a respectable number of reprintings before it went out of print.

When my friends, Sylvia and Abe Burack, the proprietors of *The Writer*, asked me to revise the text and I had committed myself to rereading my youthful pronouncements, I realized how greatly the publishing world has changed since I wrote that book. The enormous revival in reading which began with the return to campus of the G.I.'s in 1946 and has been further amplified by their children who are now in college; the rising and intensified interest in non-fiction, in works of history, foreign affairs and social science; the blizzard of paperbacks of which Americans are now purchasing upwards of 380 million copies annually, and the high costs

of the hard-cover book which have narrowed the opportunity for the new author, changes like these have compelled me to write about a very different set of circumstances from those I perceived when I entered the literary field in 1923, and what began as a revision soon came to be a fresh book. Throughout I have addressed myself to the second person plural, meaning to identify by the pronoun "you" that innumerable army of amateurs stretching from those who begin to write in college to those who have gone back to it again in mid-life or retirement. I want to facilitate their approach, to help them look realistically at their subject matter, to suggest where they may break into print, and the obstacles they must clear on their way to becoming a freelance.

My text owes much to the constructive and vigilant suggestions of Phoebe-Lou Adams and the cheerful efficiency of Beverly Yankee.

Edward Weeks

## ACKNOWLEDGMENTS

The author is indebted to a number of writers and associates whose wise comments have helped to point up his text, especially to Harry Golden, F.P.A., Alfred A. Knopf, James Thurber, Carl Brandt, Charles W. Morton, E. B. White, Ray Long, R. L. Duffus, and Paul Gallico. Many thanks are also due to Alfred A. Knopf for permission to quote from Arthur Machen's reminiscences, *Far-Off Things*; to the Outlet Book Company, Inc. for permission to quote from Ray Long's *Twenty Best Short Stories*; to the *Fortnightly* for permission to quote from their article, "The Task of the Publisher's Reader," by Frank Swinnerton; to *Sports Illustrated* for permission to quote from Gerald Holland's article on Ron Delany.

# ❧ CONTENTS

# BREAKING INTO PRINT

# I

*BEGINNER'S LUCK*

JAMES FENIMORE COOPER, a gentleman farmer in upstate New York, so the story goes, enjoyed reading the *Waverley Novels* aloud to his wife. Shipments of books were sent to him regularly from London, and on one occasion, when Sir Walter Scott was missing, Mr. Cooper tried his luck with some fiction by an unknown author. He had not gone many pages before he slammed the book shut in disgust. "Why, I could write you a better story than that myself!" he exploded. "Well, why *don't* you?" replied that gentle voice which he recognized as authority. And from this impulse his writing began. There are, of course, many such impulses that lead people to commit themselves on paper. It may be, as in Cooper's case, a reaction from a wretched book; it may be in emulation of a good one, or, more commonly, it may be the need of money; the urge may come to you while shaving in the morning or midway in a sleepless night, but whatever the cause, the idea

of writing a story, a novel, an article, or a poem occurs to almost every literate person at least once in a lifetime.

For each beginner who tries to write and who in the end proves himself a writer, there are hundreds who, after some futile scribbling, abandon the idea in despair. This is merciful for the spruce trees from which our books are made. Most beginners despair, it seems to me, first, because they really don't know how to begin, and secondly, because, even if they finish, they don't have much luck with their offerings. Which leads me to wonder if in this case "luck" is not a synonym for persistence. It is a curious truth that the most persistent people in all industry are commonly thought to be the laziest—I mean writers.

Since writing is unquestionably the worst paid of all professions, those who do it have to be persistent if they are to survive. Of this the beginner soon becomes painfully aware. In no other business I can think of is an apprentice's work so repeatedly thrown back in his face. In all fairness, however, it should be added that most beginning writers invite this treatment, not only because their writing is probably inadequate, but also because—whatever its potential value—they so seldom know where or how to get it published.

If I were a book agent, I should not spend much time trying to sell Rabelais to a Sunday School; yet this proposition is no more absurd than the disappointed

**4**

efforts of a thousand new writers whose manuscripts fly back like homing pigeons. To make a name for one's self in contemporary literature it is essential to discover as rapidly as possible the kind of thing one is best equipped to write, and then the medium—any medium —in which it can be published to advantage. Self-knowledge is slow to come by. A would-be poet who has tasted nothing but rejection may switch, as did James Norman Hall, to travel articles, which were published, and then to fiction in which he became an expert. A born poet like Stephen Vincent Benét may have to struggle to write short stories to support himself until at last a Guggenheim Fellowship grants him the two years of freedom in which to complete his big epic, *John Brown's Body*. Only by persistence, patient experiment and self-knowledge can a beginner find his medium, and his readers. Or you may, in the end, discover that you are not cut out to be a writer, and that realization, grimly and grudgingly arrived at, is far healthier than self-delusion.

By a kind of rough classification the society of writers may be divided into two communities—those who dwell in ivory towers, and those who live next to the sweat-shops. There is not much love lost between them. The ivory tower dwellers, who are most at home on the

college campus, are scornful of the sweatshoppers because of their prolific and commercial output; whereas, naturally enough, those who make their living by writing are at heart contemptuous of those who won't take the risk of being a freelance. Most beginners are members of the ivory tower set, but, as their work progresses and they become better known, they are tempted to climb off their perch and join the toilers.

It hardly needs to be said that he who lives in an ivory tower writes fastidiously and for the few. And this is as it should be, up to the point where the craftsman, for his own satisfaction, feels impelled to show his work to others. Usually he singles out those friends who, as he explains, are best qualified to judge his manuscript. They give it as their opinion that what he has written is not a bit worse—well, as a matter of fact, is a good deal better than something they saw the other day in *Horizon* or *Esquire* (or the *Atlantic*), and if an editor will pay good money, etc., etc. The writer promptly sends his manuscript to the indicated haven, and in about ninety-eight cases out of a hundred it is as promptly declined. When this experience has been repeated three or four times, your ivory tower writer begins to look down sourly on the publishing world.

You should be cautioned that your friends will invariably express pleasure in what you have written. This

does not always mean that they like it: it means that they have searched for something complimentary to say, out of regard for your feelings; it may mean that they lack the critical ability to analyze exactly what is wrong. Criticism that is at once constructive and unsparing is what beginners need and have the hardest time finding. Meantime remember that no work has been fairly tested until it has been passed on by the qualified and unbiased reader and has stood the severe scrutiny of print. To see your work in cold, inerasable type; to realize how sturdily—or how meagrely!—the words convey your meaning; to hear a stranger praise or disparage your screed—this is an experience that gets in the blood, inflames the mind, and infects you, at least temporarily, with the desire to go on writing.

It is not so difficult to break into print. True, the odds are formidable that you won't *sell* your first story to one of the higher-paying magazines that publish fiction, or your first article to one of the "quality" magazines— the *Atlantic*, *Harper's* or *The New Yorker*. Beginners must try any door that will open. Since time immemorial, retired British colonels have written letters to the *London Times*. In their critical, demanding way, they established a tradition in journalism; every daily of consequence has its letter columns today. And it might surprise you to learn how far a letter in the *New York Times* will throw its gleam, if the correspondent gener-

ates light as well as heat—in short, gives evidence of knowing what he is talking about. A fresh opinion vigorously pressed is a godsend to the journalist making up the editorial page, and it is fair to say that a good many magazine articles have originated in the columns of correspondence.

In American newspapers, on the same editorial page that reprints the letters, or on a facing page, you are likely to find another popular feature, a column of salty comments, local color and perhaps some light verse. When I was breaking in, the best columns in New York City were run by Christopher Morley in the New York *Evening Post*, by Heywood Broun in the *World* and by Franklin P. Adams ("F.P.A.") in the *Tribune*. In "The Conning Tower," for instance, F.P.A. printed his own Manhattan diary after the manner of Pepys; he made some fine-edged translations of Horace; he was constantly deriding other publications for their sloppy use of English, and day after day he printed the sketches, witticisms and light verse of new writers. Each year he presented a gold watch to the beginner who had served him best, and Gelett Burgess, Dorothy Parker, Deems Taylor, Louis Untermeyer and Robert Benchley are five of the many who won those watches. "I was not doing favors for these boys," F.P.A. once wrote me, "the favors were on the other foot."

Today the importance of political commentators in

the metropolitan dailies and our concern for foreign policy tend to crowd out this more relaxed light-hearted journalism, but such columns are still very much alive in the local press. They speak in the idiom and color of a region and not infrequently they give space to a beginner. For many years, Ben Hur Lampman was the authentic, kindly voice of the Pacific Northwest in his very popular column in *The Oregonian*. He wrote about an old dog named Blinker, of a zany old woman who lived at the end of the carline, or he set down the cantankerous banter and affection of Him and Her as they sit jawing in the kitchen. Lampman's prose was as fresh run as the water of the Columbia used to be.

You will find the liveliest columns in those regions where big change is in progress. If the local newspaper turns a deaf ear to your appeal, perhaps there is a trade journal that will let you in, or a resort guide, published during the summer, which would be the gayer for your jottings. If all avenues seem closed, you may have to find a way to establish a sheet of your own. This is what Harry Golden did in Charlotte, North Carolina—Harry who began life on the top floor of a cold-water tenement on the East Side of New York. "I wanted to publish a liberal newspaper in North Carolina," he wrote, "but I was a Jew, a liberal, and a northerner. The odds were too much. So I insulated myself. I called the paper *The Carolina Israelite*. My

critics would say, 'This is another Jew paper,' and perhaps, I thought, sooner or later, the non-Jews would get acquainted with it."

In the columns of his paper, which was launched in October 1942, he found his way of saying unaggressively the sage, firm things that needed to be said, clearly and understandingly, about the deep-set emotional crisis in the South. It was natural and honorable that a Jew who had known deprivation should write in such sympathy with the Negroes who were being deprived. The country responded to his humor and his disarming reasonableness as it once had to Will Rogers. His three books of short essays, *Only in America, For 2¢ Plain,* and *Enjoy, Enjoy,* have been bought and taken to heart by more than two million readers, and except for a dozen pieces which were written specifically for the third volume, the entire contents came straight from the columns of *The Carolina Israelite.*

There is another door to journalism which can be opened by the persistent, especially by those who are willing to be printed without pay. Many of our metropolitan newspapers maintain a "book page": the best of these papers publish book reviews every day and on Sundays; the second-best put the page together once a week, and in view of the phenomenal increase in reading sparked by the younger generation during the past

ten years, even the small-town papers may be reaching for a book review editor in the near future.

The problem of the book review editor is how to cope with the twelve thousand or more new books, reprints and paperbacks which are turned out each year by the publishers. He will be expected to write appropriate chitchat about the authors and quotable reviews about the more deserving volumes; since this is a bigger assignment than one man can handle (Henry L. Mencken in the great days of *The American Mercury* did *all* the book reviews in addition to editing the magazine, but he was the exception), most reviewers farm out their surplus books to other members of the editorial staff or to friends outside. The honorarium is modest. I know of one paper which pays the sub-reviewer $1.00 a book, but insists that the review copy be returned so that it may be sold to a second-hand dealer. The more general practice is to give the sub-reviewer the book *and* the pleasure of seeing his copy in print. *The Saturday Review of Literature* and *The New York Times Book Review* and *The Herald-Tribune Books*, which are in effect magazines, pay quite respectable fees and are not easily accessible to the newcomer. Read them and aspire to be in them, but don't make your bid until you have had quite a thorough try-out in your local paper with the clippings to show for it.

It is obvious that all reviewers like to see themselves

11

quoted in publishers' advertisements—a natural vanity and besides it keeps one in good odor with the boss— and this being so, it is tempting to take a book as you find it in the blurb and to slop over into those catch-words which have lost all freshness. It is so easy to say that the characters in a novel are "convincing"; that a biography is "full-bodied"; a detective story "intri-guing"; and a novel of love "warmly endearing". The late William Lyon Phelps, a popular professor at Yale who stimulated the reading of many but who allowed himself to be quoted too often, used one stock phrase among many others—that John Galsworthy "was in the very plenitude of his powers"; this jarred on me so the first two times I read it that I have tried to keep away from such toffee-words ever after.

In your copy avoid the shopworn, avoid the tempting sales talk the publisher has printed on the jacket, and above all, avoid superlatives. The chances are that you won't have much chance to use the latter at the outset, for the books you will be given will be of humbler order.

"Can you give me anything to review?" asked a friend of mine as she presented herself at the office of the *Hartford Courant*. "First novels? Anything."

"You mean you're not going to hold out for master-pieces?" said the review editor laconically.

"Anything," she repeated.

And that is what she got, books for children, travel

books, first novels—anything that needed doing. It is the way to begin.

Four paragraphs or five hundred words are about what you will be given for the average inconspicuous review, and working at that length you must be concise and careful to avoid the two most obvious verbosities: use only enough biographical detail to explain why the author is qualified—if he is—to handle his subject; and secondly, remember that it is your function to suggest, to give the flavor of the book, but not to give it all away. The woman in the row behind you at the theatre who has seen the show before and thinks she must warn her companion of what is to come is no more of a bore than the reviewer who devotes most of his space to a skeleton-ized digest of the plot. People read for a variety of reasons. They read fiction to be amused, to be surprised and to be stirred. It is deadening to everyone's interest —reader, author and publisher—to see the contents of a promising new novel (which has taken the author ten months to write) predigested in four paragraphs by a hack.

I like the two-pronged approach. Tell us first what it is the author has tried to do. A reviewer must define the nature of a book, he must give us a feeling for it before he comes to his judgment. Most novelists are working on two levels: the narrative as it develops on the surface, and the inner conflict as it takes possession of the minds

13

and hearts of the characters. The deeper theme, so often these days symbolic of our precarious state, is the more devious and the more difficult for the reviewer to cope with in limited space. When you think you have discerned the intent, then tell us how well you think the author has managed his material—where is he at his best, his second-best, where vulnerable? Has he a true ear for dialogue? Does he force the pace or depend too much on coincidence? Has his satire a cutting edge; if he is given to symbolism and analogy, does his meaning come through? Or if it be a work of non-fiction, is it well documented? (Henry Mencken was always looking for an index: he thought every self-respecting history or biography should have one.) Does the interest in it build up steadily and, this being an age of specialization, is there a category of readers for whom this book will be particularly meaningful?

These are not questions the reviewer can answer by skimming. I need a minimum of four hours in which to review all but the shortest volumes, and as I read, I make quite a few reading notes in the blank white pages at the back. A book of such absorbing detail as *The Armada* by Garrett Mattingly took me the better part of two weekends, and my notes and quotable passages filled three full pages of cramped writing. Not till you are a professional can you review on the run. At the peak of his vitality, Arnold Bennett reviewed on an average of

three hundred novels a year, fitting the work as he said "into the odd unoccupied corners of my time, the main portions of which are given to the manufacture of novels, plays, short stories, and longer literary essays." He was writing a million words a year when he made that remark, and his familiarity with the elements and structure of fiction reduced his book reviewing to a form of swift exercise. I doubt if he read page-by-page one book in fifty.

Our esteem for the unsigned reviews in *The Times Literary Supplement* (London) prompts us to think that English criticism is of a higher order than our own. Actually this was not the case when I entered publishing, nor is it today. I can remember the time when a "lit'ry figger," call him Clarence Meredith-Jones, would receive a substantial fee from a London publisher for editing a diamond-in-the-rough novel, and five months later would unabashedly accept other fees for reviewing the same book in not one, but as many as three, different papers. That he was playing favorites never seemed to trouble him, but he did have the shrewdness to sign his reviews with different initials in each case. I doubt if such log rolling would be tolerated in London today. I notice other changes which are in the right direction: British critics are no longer as condescending as they once were in their attitude toward American scholars, and especially toward those scholars who are working

15

on English subjects. And we for our part no longer regard English writers as having a heaven-sent priority in
fiction and poetry. All this makes for a healthier ex-
change, especially in the field of literary criticism.

The besetting weakness among American reviewers is
the tendency to over-praise. In my first year on the
staff of the *Atlantic*, I saw a good deal of my friend and
former roommate at Harvard, William Whitman III,
an associate editor at Houghton Mifflin Co. with duties
somewhat analogous to mine as a first reader at the
*Atlantic*. Miss Amy Lowell, the sister of the Harvard
President, was then a powerful figure in poetry, the
leader of the Imagists, a practitioner of free verse, a
friend of Ezra Pound, and a benefactor to many younger
struggling poets. Before the publication of what was to
be her final volume of verse, my friend Bill went out to
interview her for the *Boston Evening Transcript*, and
after he had written his piece, he went out again with
the proofs to see if Miss Lowell approved of what he
had said. Having been trained in the good Harvard tradition of never using a superlative, Bill constantly referred to Miss Lowell as "one of the pioneers . . . one
of the most versatile, etc.," but when the proofs were
returned to him, he noticed that the comparatives had
all been turned into superlatives by the poet herself.

It is natural for authors to want to be praised and
natural that their publishers should indulge them by

16

doing so. But not all. Alfred A. Knopf is one of the few who can look objectively at his own books as well as at those of his competitors. In his article "Book Publishing: The Changes I've Seen," which we published in the *Atlantic* for December 1957, he remarked, "A single publisher announces for one season '12 superb new novels.' I suppose it would be a good season that produced two or three novels to which the adjective *superb* could legitimately be applied." Later in that same piece he went on to say:

> I would like to speak briefly about reviewers. When I was young, a good many people were around who could really get a hearing for a book: William Lyon Phelps at Yale, at whom the intellectuals used to laugh but whose enthusiasms were really contagious; Henry L. Mencken, who could even sell a book by denouncing it, so arresting was his invective; Heywood Broun in New York; Henry Sell, Burton Rascoe, and Fanny Butcher in Chicago, and many others. Today book reviewers seem to have fallen on poor times. I think only Orville Prescott writing in the *New York Times* can convey effectively his enthusiasm for a new book to a considerable number of readers and make them buy a book he praises. We would all benefit enormously were there a dozen like him.

As Mr. Knopf well says, there is an open field for those who can write about books with discrimination and enthusiasm. My last advice to those intent upon re-

17

viewing is this: Practice humility in your approach to a book and when you give your judgment about it. Look for the best that is in the text and put what you find in balance. Try not to be didactic, and remember that none of us is infallible. When Clifton Fadiman was doing his weekly reviews for *The New Yorker,* he wrote with verve and discrimination, and he covered a wide range of titles. Invariably toward the year's end he would devote an entire article to reassessing his earlier judgments of that year, specifying those books about which he had been overgenerous in his praise and those which had proved to be better than he first thought. This is what I mean by humility, and if you are working in that vein, you will be prompted to avoid superlatives. A Shakespeare, a Keats, a Dylan Thomas or a Hemingway does not recur every ten years.

It is sad but true that practically all beginning writers have to support themselves at another trade. I shall want to amplify this point later, but since I have been talking about newspapers and such piecework as they can give a beginner, let me state now quite positively that of all the trades available, journalism offers you the swiftest and best training for writing, and that if you are one of the few who are picked to work on the sports page, you are fortunate indeed. I never got that far, but I aspired to. As an undergraduate for two years I covered Harvard for the *Boston Evening Transcript,*

and during my graduate study in England I wrote special articles both for the *Transcript* and for my hometown paper, the *Elizabeth Daily Journal*. When I began searching for jobs in the hot summer of 1923, I turned naturally to the offices of the *New York Tribune*, the daily which my family had always read. "Don't let them put you on the copy desk," said my friends on the staff. "Try to get on the sports page or on the street." Mr. Mason, the Managing Editor, listened to me patiently and finally hired me as a cub reporter in sports. But when I reported early on a Monday morning I found that all the cubs, and I among them, had been lopped off as a result of the merger with the *New York Herald*. So I was fired from this job before I ever began.

A sports writer has what every great writer of action must have, a kind of split vision. I can best describe what I mean when I think of Bill Tilden who was the best tennis player this country has produced. Tilden played with enormous concentration. He could take the fastest serve on the rise, and while with one pair of eyes he was timing his return, with the other pair he was watching where his opponent had moved. If he rushed the net, Tilden would pass him; if he stayed back, Tilden drove him out of position. All good writers of action operate with two sets of eyes, one for the immediate scene, the other for the background: while they are taking in the double-play or the long forward pass, they

are also spotting the reaction of the referee who may have been caught out of position, or the spontaneous protest of the crowd who have sensed an illegal interference. The roster of sports writers who have gone on to bigger things is a lustrous one, and for our time it includes Ring Lardner and his greatest admirer Ernest Hemingway, John Kieran, Heywood Broun, Paul Gallico and James B. Reston, to name but a few.

The sports page has long been an excellent proving ground for men who go on to do brilliant work in exposition or in fiction, and if today you read the columns of Red Smith, who is to our generation what Grantland Rice was to his a generation earlier, you will see why. The sports page gives you the opportunity of calling the shots as you see them and more freely than any other department in a great newspaper, it gives you the opportunity to do so in a style which is your own and just as amusing, just as indignant, and just as individual as you can make it. No one in the United States, no judge on the bench, no moralist or satirist has ever written as witheringly about the corruption in professional prize-fighting or as appreciatively about the courage of a jockey like Eddie Arcaro, as Red Smith.

To the few of inner aspiration on the sports page a question in time will present itself: when can I become less of a journalist and more of a writer? A man may have to live with this question for some time. In 1917

Ernest Hemingway served his apprenticeship on the *Kansas City Star* and after the war, when he had recovered from his wounds, he wrote for space as a foreign correspondent for the *Toronto Star*. It was Gertrude Stein who took upon herself the credit for shaking him loose from such semi-security. "Stop doing those articles," she said to him, in effect. "It is time you gave your undivided attention to your stories." It may, indeed, have been her elbow in his ribs which jolted him, but even without it he would have freed himself. The process of how you work your way into the clear is different for every beginner, and it is fortuitous. No one has touched upon this latter element more delightfully than Paul Gallico in the introduction which he wrote for one of his more famous stories, "The Roman Kid." His words are so telling, they hold out such hope for other beginners, that I should like to quote them *in extenso:*

Back in 1933 the *Daily News* sent me to Rome to negotiate with the Italian Government of Benito Mussolini for a team of Italian amateur boxers to come to the United States and fight our New York Golden Gloves team in an international match at the Yankee Stadium.

The party big shots kept me cooling my heels for weeks while trying to make up their minds whether the Fascist State could afford to let the representatives of the new Italian Empire be mussed up by a gang of degenerate New York democrats. While waiting, I

used my spare time to do some research in libraries and museums and at the American Academy to see if I could find out what was actually known about sports in ancient Rome.

During this time I met Professor Prentice Duell, the brilliant Harvard archaeologist, who was likewise living at the Hotel Ambasciatori, and we formed a lasting friendship. . . This was a tough young guy. I admired him a lot and he guided me in my research work.

He took me to Tarquinia to see the wonderful frescoes on the walls of the Etruscan tombs, to the Colosseum and the Forum Romano, and one day he suggested we go to the Museo delle Terme in Rome, near the old thermal baths, to look at the recently exhumed statue known as the *Sitting Boxer*.

This proved to be a truly wonderful life-size bronze of an ancient bearded Roman gladiator, a boxer, his hands armed with the lethal iron cesti, the Roman version of the boxing glove, which were laced to his hands with bronze reproductions of the leather thongs that crisscrossed his forearms to the elbow. He was seated and there were wounds to be seen, extraordinarily vivid delineations of the wear and tear that comes to a fighter during the course of a rough evening. . .

Now, to a sports editor and veteran boxing writer who had seen many hundreds of professional and amateur fights and boxing matches, the statue and the condition of the old pugil's face and arms and body spoke volumes. Every muscle, his attitude,

his hands, the battered ears, and the marks on his features told their story, a story that anyone who had spent as many hours as I at the ringside and in the dressing-rooms of fighters before and after matches could read.

For days I had been sitting literally at Duell's feet, popeyed at his erudition and knowledge of antiquity, drinking in the wisdom he had excavated from the ages. Now for the first time I was confronted with a situation where I knew a lot of things he didn't know, and the temptation to show off to him a little was too great to resist. With somewhat studied casualness I said:

"Well, now, I can't tell you anything about the period to which it belongs or the artist who made it, but I can tell you a little about the big guy himself, what he was like and how he fought, and maybe even something about the chap who mussed him up."

Then I proceeded to do so with excellent results, for now Prentice's eyes bugged; he was the impressed student and I the erudite professor, for a moment anyway, expounding the deeply scientific lore of scrambling ears. . . .

It wasn't until five years later, while I was working as a feature writer for International News Service and wanted passage money to get back to England in the spring, that I thought of using the idea of the *Sitting Boxer* in a short story.

There is the origin of "The Roman Kid," a story which probably more than any other helped to liberate

and establish Paul Gallico as a narrator. It took five years to germinate and when at last he wrote it he used himself as a model, and for the hero he chose Tommy Thompson, a friend of his, a sports writer for the *Daily Blade* who had gone to Spain as a war correspondent and there been killed. "It's queer," Gallico adds, "what things come out when you set out to put an idea into story framework."

# II

## 𝒩 THE ARTICLE

In the past decade we discovered to our surprise that despite the distractions of television and the long-playing record, the American people were devoting more time to books than ever before in this century. This revolution in reading was ignited by the veterans who came back to college at the end of the Second World War hungry for education; it has been kept going ever since by the undergraduates, and that it will be redoubled in the near future seems probable as we scan the sharp upcurve in our college communities, the result of our rising birth rate.

This rejuvenation of interest in books, most noticeable in readers under forty-five, was facilitated by the development of the paperback. Publishers experimented in the years 1939-1945, and when at first the flood gates were opened, the vast majority of paperbacks (leaving aside the juveniles) were novels tricked out with lurid jackets and were devoted to sex, sadism and murder.

25

But what is significant editorially is that the pendulum of public taste has quietly been swinging away from this fiction and toward the field of serious, factual non-fiction. This swing is partly to be explained by the dearth of good novelists and short story writers—it is harder to write fiction today than it used to be—but mainly, I think, by the temper of the public. To a degree it reflects the anxiety of the country, the conscientiousness of the individual reader and his need for information, guidance, and reassurance. I look for it to continue.

The point of departure can, I believe, be traced back to the year 1934 when the New Deal was beginning to regulate and improvise a way out of the depression; when Hitler was building up his ascendancy; when Spain was on the verge of civil war; and when we were last among the great powers to recognize the Soviet Union. Then, as Mrs. Katharine Fullerton Gerould pointed out in her article in *The Saturday Review of Literature*, "people found themselves immensely uninformed on a vast number of subjects that had suddenly grown important." This need to be informed has helped to shelve the essay (which I shall discuss later), and it has provided article writers and foreign correspondents with a far larger readership than they could ever have commanded in the 1920's. Hitler's triumph at Munich, the Axis Pact, the collapse of France, our own vulnerability at Pearl Harbor, the experience of total war,

Hiroshima, the knowledge in 1949 that we were now in a nuclear arms race with Russia, Korea, the belligerency of Red China, the crumbling of Western empires, the exploration of Space—these are the ponderables that swept away every last bastion of American isolation. Today we are all in the same boat, more exposed than we like, doing our best on a turbulent sea to steer by the stars.

All through these recurring crises, the demand for information was far greater than what was available. College professors and scientists from what Jacques Barzun called "The Ivory Lab" were called out of their obscurity—the scientists have stated their case with striking effect in *The Bulletin of the Atomic Scientists* —and in editorial offices there was a year-round search for staff writers and experienced contributors who could think critically, cover their subject and document their findings.

There are never enough qualified and articulate critics available *in any field*, and in the period of ferment I am describing, this lack became painfully noticeable in Big Business and in Labor, in Science, Psychology and Social Science, to name but five. The presidents of our largest corporations have one thing in common with the presidents of our most powerful unions: both officials are too busy to speak for themselves, and they delegate their writing to staff economists or public

27

relations officers. For every Clarence Randall of Inland Steel or Leland Hazard of Pittsburgh Plate Glass, there are ten whose ghost-written material reads as if it were written in soft soap. The boys in the sciences, on the other hand, do speak for themselves but in trade language of their own devising, a gobbledygook to which they become so habituated that they fail to communicate half of what they seek to tell the laymen.

In view of these deficiencies, let me say now what perhaps I should have said earlier. Given this ferment in the world, given the most ruthless competition for readers that has ever existed in the magazine industry, how absurd it is for anyone to assume that manuscripts by the unknown are not read and read intently: The stream which flows in to the *Atlantic* is larger than at any time in our history, and to cope with it we have our first readers, the best we can get and ranging in age so that they touch the various generations. But, in fact, all of us read—the managing editor, the associate editor, the head copy-editor, the publisher (when he can spare time), and myself. As the old adage says, you don't have to eat the whole of an egg to know that it is bad. No, but you have to eat enough. And in place of that shopworn figure I should like to put this: Several of our competitors—*The New Yorker* for one— pay larger fees than we can afford, and what is more, place their contributors, not infrequently beckoned

away from us, under a first-refusal contract. Our only answer to that is to live by our discoveries—which in fact we have been doing ever since we went into business in November 1857. Some of our discoveries have been quite famous—and the only way to discover new talent is to read it.

To judge manuscripts requires about equal parts of curiosity and decisiveness. By curiosity I mean an eager, unflagging interest in the written word which sends you from one Manila envelope to another with perpetual hope and holds you fast to a discouraging paper till you are sure there is not a redeeming feature in it. Such curiosity is only human: it is keen and more critical in the morning, a time I used as a first reader to absorb myself in the articles, the controversy, the books of history and biography from which it was hoped we would cut an excerpt for the magazine; it is more kindly disposed after lunch, which I found an agreeable time for stories. As I advanced in rank, it became necessary for me to take home a larger burden of reading, and today I do most of it at night and during the reflective hours of the weekend. With the poetry folder open on my lap, I can read poet against poet to find the difference and balance that we need, or story after story to make sure that we do not overdo the didactic—so many have to do with race relations!—or themes darkly shadowed by death.

29

Editing is a ceaseless business of making decisions, and the attrition can be very fatiguing. I remember that at the dinner announcing my appointment as Editor, Bliss Perry gave me this smiling admonition: "Remember how vulnerable we all are to indigestion. When you're feeling bilious try to defer your difficult decisions to the next day." Yes, and for this reason or because we still see hope, we sometimes defer a decision for weeks. But five hundred acceptances out of an annual submission of 45,000 manuscripts will give you some idea of the odds, and when the decisions—alas, so preponderantly negative—are final, those we cannot use must be dispatched with polite, impersonal notes beginning, "We have read with interest your manuscript . . . but we regret that it is unsuitable for our purpose . . ."

I have been describing the conditions under which articles are written and submitted, and now what constructive advice can I give those who are trying to get a hearing?

The preponderance of our non-fiction comes from men, and for the reasons I have suggested, the tone and substance have become progressively more serious. Humor, the lighthearted American way of distorting and exaggerating the prosaic, was one of the first casualties of the cold war. Our articles now are more

30

likely to be the prompting of conscience, and the vigilance and sincerity with which the unsolicited male contributors devote themselves to the major problems of our day is heartening. In certain months, notably the autumn, were we given paper and a subsidy, we could put out a secondary issue of the *Atlantic* which would be perhaps 75 per cent as readable as the one we printed. But inevitably it would go over a great deal of the same ground.

The pity of it is that there should be so much duplication in all this endeavor. Survival is the one insistent theme, and it hammers away through thousands of papers on Communism, disarmament, and our chances of besting the Soviet Union in economic competition. They come from sober minds and from those acting on impulse; they are supposed, of course, to be documented, but that does not deter people who really know little about history, power-politics, Marxism or modern weapons from writing reams about how we can (a) arrange peace with the Soviet Union, or (b) blow her to hell and gone with the Springfield rifle. If you are contemplating a world shaker such as this, study the last three issues of the magazine to which you propose to sell it to be sure that you have not been anticipated, and then ask yourself if what you are prepared to say is simply your opinion (one man, one vote) or whether it can be based on facts and argued with enough

31

authority to sway others. If you are in any doubt, send the editor a two-page outline of what you have in mind to see if he is sympathetic; if he is not, you have saved yourself time and effort.

The belligerency of the recurring crises in which we live will force out of the more conscientious the pleas and protests and proposals for a settlement short of desolation. Every editor respects this and yet every editor knows that the judgment of foreign policy or disarmament calls for the experience and wisdom of experts like George F. Kennan or Walter Lippmann or Edward Crankshaw. In the inexorable competition for a hearing, the amateur, the unknown, will find the odds against him, and so, I repeat, he should resort to the letter, either to sound out a magazine editor or to see if his views merit the serious consideration of the letters column in the Sunday *New York Times*.

There is a widespread belief among article writers that if a foreign area has sprung into sudden notice, everything about it is worthy of attention. Acting on this fallacy, a hopeful contributor will send us a manuscript with a letter beginning, "Since you have just published Sir Winston Churchill's account of his visit to Luxembourg, I thought you might like to read these reminiscences of my grandfather who went to that little country in 1892. Your readers may enjoy the comparison . . ." Dozens of such memoirs of Cuba emerged

from the attic when Castro began his rampage, and hundreds of others have been released by the upheavals in Africa. But there is an axiom in journalism that the present always comes first.

We have been speaking of subjects which are charged with controversy. Here, it seems to me, the beginner has his best chance if he can present an aspect of American life which he knows right down to the ground. In many small towns in the northeast, the rivalry between the high schools and the parochial schools for both pupils and dollars is serious enough to give parents anxiety. What do you know about it? In Kentucky, strip mining, one of the worst regulated of our transient industries, is defacing fine forest slopes with the aim of producing cheap coal for sale to the TVA. This is a mockery of conservation—and what do you know about it? Baltimore and New Haven, thanks to enlightenment in their city halls, have cleaned up their traffic and urban renewal problems—where does your home town stand? Has gambling become an irresistibly corrosive force in American life? What happens when $2.00 bets by the million flow into the narcotic ring? A liberal led revolution in New York City tossed out the bosses of Tammany: How did it begin at the grass roots and who pushed it through? If power dams and industrial pollution continue at their present rate on the West Coast, how long will the Pacific salmon survive? If we

33

raise compulsory school attendance to the age of eighteen, what effect will it have on juvenile delinquency? If we have not enough recreation areas for our population of today, how can we possibly secure enough for our citizens with the shorter work-week of 1976? These questions and others like them go to the fabric of our society, democracy as it is being lived, not dreamed. They must be answered by citizens who are alert and not afraid to dig up the facts.

There is one brief postscript to all this that I ought to mention. If you have been provoked into action by what some other writer has published, bear in mind that the manuscript stating your rebuttal and putting forward your own case should be posted with the least possible delay. The manufacturing problem of sustaining a running controversy in successive numbers of a magazine is so difficult that few editors will bother with it. Your only chance is to get in fast.

I have said that men predominate in writing articles, but this does not mean that they have a monopoly or necessarily do it better. I have found that a woman who excels in article writing is likely to be very conscientious with evidence and statistics; this is notably true of both Agnes E. Meyer and Barbara Ward. When Agnes de Mille writes on the question of whether a woman who is an artist can also be a good wife and

mother, she is not using figures but she is drawing on her extraordinarily wide and sensitive knowledge of the theatre and the ballet. When Nora Johnson, an *Atlantic* novelist and a graduate of Smith College, wrote at our suggestion an article on "Sex and the College Girl", she was drawing not only on what she remembered from Northampton, but on what she had learned as a young wife and writer living in Manhattan. The response to her findings was so widespread and corroborative that two years later we urged Mrs. Johnson to do a second piece for us on "The Captivity of Marriage", telling of the overburden of children, housekeeping, and a little money-earning on the side, which so many young college wives find themselves contending with, and again the commenting letters told us she had hit her target. These were the first two articles she had ever published.

In the 1920's when the country was enjoying life, editors had to engender controversy out of Prohibition, the rising divorce rates, and the antics of Flaming Youth. Today the world is so full of unsolved—and insoluble—problems that the shoe is on the other foot: we have to search far and wide for enough entertainment and amenity to balance the headaches. One perennially pleasant subject is food. So much of it now comes to us canned, cooked, sealed, processed and with the best of the taste removed that good writing about good cooking never fails to attract a hungry audience.

In Della T. Lutes we found a veteran who knew how old-fashioned American cooking ought to be done. She had the recipes, and she wrote of salt-rising bread and deep-dish apple pie and chocolate cake with a dash of ground-up cloves, and pig's knuckles and oyster stew in a way to make your mouth water. What she did was to tell us short stories, beginning and ending in her mother's kitchen, with one succulent dish accurately described in each—and a legion of our women readers went out to try it Della's way.

Akin to this is the period piece. I take the caption from that delectable book, *Period Piece*, which Gwen Raverat wrote about her girlhood in the Charles Darwin circle in Cambridge, and it is equally applicable to Thomas Barbour's account of his boyhood in Eau Gallie, his grandmother's estate in Florida, as he tells of it in *That Vanishing Eden*. Our way of living has changed so fast in this century that things which were commonplace in the early 1900's now seem quaint, historic—and laughable. Reginald Washburn, a one-time director of the *Atlantic*, told me that when he and his bride were married in 1903, they planned to begin their honeymoon by motoring from the Hotel Victoria in Boston to the Groton Inn, a distance of thirty-eight miles, in a two-cylinder buckboard. "Two cylinders," he explained, "so in case one broke down we'd have the other to fall back on." Well, that is precisely what

happened: One cylinder began to stutter shortly after they left Boston, and for the remaining thirty miles they jerked along in a lugubrious way that gave them each a painfully stiff neck. Such episodes well and truthfully recalled are priceless. Old cars, old bicycle trips, old bathing suits, old motorboats that sputtered and died—the field is limitless, if you were there and have a good memory. "My father," wrote John Reese, "worked in the sale barns in Grand Island, Nebraska, when that was the largest horse market in the world. Before that he had served in the cavalry in the Philippines and had trained horses for ranchers and horse brokers. Dad was a horseman 'by trade.' " And with that beginning, Mr. Reese went on to write for the *Atlantic* (July 1961) "That's Why I Still Miss Horses", a piece so full of the savor, the beauty, and the power of fine horseflesh that one reads it with tears of laughter and nostalgia.

One cannot dissect the anatomy of humor, nor will there ever be a formula for writing it. For what strikes one person as hilarious will leave another cold. All we can say is that some writers, James Thurber and Clarence Day, for instance, are blessed with the facility to make many people laugh. The number of writers who can do this is limited in any generation.

At the time of Will Rogers' death in 1935, two rich and traditional sources of American comedy were drying up. Magazines which fostered humor, the old *Life*,

*Puck, Judge* and *College Humor,* had all suspended publication, and the rather sophisticated humor which once found its way into Frank Crowninshield's *Vanity Fair* was now appearing with fresh accents in *The New Yorker.* The accents of *The New Yorker* are not easy to emulate. Sophisticated and sardonic with a swift power of suggestion, they set an example which few beginners can cope with. *The New Yorker* style is only one of many ways in which to be funny, but those who cannot manage it are nowadays somewhat at a loss where to go.

At the same time that the humorous magazines were drying up, the vaudeville and burlesque circuits were losing their hold. This natural source of racy comedy which had produced Will Rogers, Fred Allen, Jack Donahue, and Jack Benny, more and more fed its bright talents into radio and television, and I suspect that to the same media today turn the young writers fresh from college and especially those with a gift for dialogue. When Herman Wouk, the novelist, and Arnold Auerbach, the dramatist, graduated from Columbia, they were immediately employed by Fred Allen, who was in need of the best help he could get for "Allen's Alley."

Humor is a scarcity in print today, and there are many editors who wish they could find more—up-country humor, East Side humor, adolescent humor, husband-and-wife humor, man-against-the-machine humor, or

children's humor. This last category, incidentally, is one of the hardest of all to write.

There is, as I have said, no formula. When James Thurber wrote about life, he wrote about it as it seemed to him. Some of it turned out to be funny, but it always had its foundation in reality. Go back and re-read the Thurber portraits of his mother and father in *The Thurber Album*. He says of his father, "He was plagued by the mechanical . . . Knobs froze at his touch, doors stuck, lines fouled, the detachable would not detach, the adjustable would not adjust. He could rarely get the top off anything, and he was forever trying to unlock something with the key to something else. In 1908, trying to fix the snap lock of the door to his sons' rabbit pen, he succeeded only after getting inside the cage, where he was imprisoned for three hours with six Belgian hares and thirteen guinea pigs." The chapter on his mother, entitled "Lavender with a Difference," is just as enchanting, and when he describes her visits to New York you see that it was the city that was capitulating to her and not the other way around.

Remember Betty MacDonald's exasperated, odds-against struggle with those chickens in her ludicrous book *The Egg and I*. There was nothing forced in that situation; she had grown to hate the chicken farm and the taste and smell and drudgery of caring for the fowl,

but she was stuck with it, and out of reality came the laughter.

In 1942 when death and destruction filled so many pages of the *Atlantic*, we decided to open a new department at the back of the magazine. We called it Accent on Living. Ever since its beginning it has been edited by my Associate Editor, Charles W. Morton, and here is how he defines his policy:

> Our hope, in the Accent on Living pages, is to offer the reader something gay and amusing, or something very odd, or a combination of these qualities. When we began the department in the July, 1942, issue, we had a few good odds and ends on hand with which to start, but no dependable contributors to whom we could turn. But what we published as we went along proved to generate new ideas and more ideas and all sorts of manuscripts from entirely new contributors. Some of them became so good that their work demanded their repeated appearances in the department, but we have always enjoyed finding new writers and new comedy and oddities.

Mr. Morton himself is one of the best humorists now writing in New England. If you want to get the real Morton flavor, read his book, *How to Protect Yourself Against Women and Other Vicissitudes*, all of which appeared in the Accent. And because he is an exceptional editor, he enjoys helping others bring their individuality into clear and delightful focus.

I think of Elinor Goulding Smith writing about her "Formal Education" and the smatterings of it that stayed with her in later life. Or of Anne Kelley, who regards herself as the perfect target for all the cold cream, soap and cosmetics advertisements, of John Gould who sends us his saturnine pieces from Maine, and of C. S. Jennison whose light verse holds all the pent-up frustration of the busy mother contending with the Younger Generation. They were all encouraged by Mr. Morton, and as I name them I realize that the way is open and that American humor, versatile, tender or wry, as you please, can be had if you look for it.

# III

## ❧ THE SHORT STORY

I HAVE HEARD it said that the short story is singularly adapted to the nervous, creative energy of the American character and that in it we are at our best. Ernest Hemingway would certainly be one of our candidates for pre-eminence, but the English could say the same for Kipling, Conrad and Somerset Maugham, so instead of claiming priority, I think we can safely settle for this: that month in, month out, more short stories are written, published—and not published—in the United States than in any other country under the sun.

Such continues to be the case despite the fact that it is so difficult to write fiction of any kind in our time. James Hilton, the English novelist and author of *Goodbye, Mr. Chips*, was a friend of mine, and I well remember our last meeting together in Hollywood, for it occurred shortly after we had learned that the Russians had perfected, far ahead of our expectation, their atomic bomb. Jimmie was depressed by the news: He

foresaw that this would involve us and all mankind in the most dangerous armament race in human history.

I knew that he was at work on a new novel, and at a favorable opening I asked about it. "Well, I've tried four beginnings," he replied. "I think I have quite a good subject, and for about a week I can keep it going. Then somewhere after page 50, it's as if the words 'So what?' suddenly spring up in capitals in the center of the page. We none of us have the confidence we once had now that we know about those bombs. This is a hard time in which to try to write." Hilton was speaking for all who devote themselves to creating and guiding character. It does take confidence—a little of what Jove had on Mount Olympus—and a great deal of discipline and sustained emotion to project and carry out a short story, much less a novel in a world as threatening and disordered as ours.

I think we will get off on the right foot if we begin with the acknowledgment that stories of any length, good stories, are harder to write than most readers will ever imagine. The exceptional craftsman—F. Scott Fitzgerald was one, Peter Ustinov is another—may have the skill to finish an acceptable story in one day of writing, but for most professionals and all amateurs, the ordeal will take much longer than that. I can only give you one generalization that may help: The more you can work at it in continuity—that is day after day,

not every second weekend—the better it will be. When you come back to an unfinished narrative after an interval, your mood may have changed and the tension vanished.

Most of us finish a piece of writing with exhilaration and relief, and probably being a bit winded, what we yearn to hear is praise followed by those rewarding words, "We are delighted to accept. . . ." In this vulnerable state, you must resist the impulse to carry your darling at considerable expense to a distant editor and read aloud choice bits of it to him. There could be no surer way of poisoning its chances. Send in your manuscript by mail; this is simple and expedient and the editors will give it a fairer trial in privacy. First and last, *a story must plead its own case.* Always keep a carbon copy, preferably two.

In May 1956, Martha Bacon, the novelist and poet who was then a member of my editorial staff, wrote an article for *The Writer* on "How to Submit a Manuscript" which is so pertinent that I should like to abridge some of her advice here:

> Don't submit the same material simultaneously to several editors. This can lead anywhere from strained relations between you and the publishing world, to out-and-out entanglement with the full majesty of the law.

44

Don't turn every other page of your manuscript upside down to find out whether your entire manuscript has really been read. The chances are that the reader will simply shift direction with you . . .

Don't write to the editor in advance, informing him you have a story or poem to submit, and asking him whether he can use it and what he will pay for it. An editor can't tell whether he can use a story or poem until he reads it. And the time to discuss payments is after the editor has made a favorable decision.

Don't bother the editor by mail or by telephone to find out if he likes your manuscript. Give him time to read it. (If you haven't heard from him in about six weeks, though, you may drop him a polite note asking if he has received the manuscript.)

Don't ask for criticism. If the editor feels he may be able to use your manuscript in his magazine, he'll tell you what he thinks of it.

Do send in legible, typewritten manuscripts. Use a good grade of standard (8½ by 11 inches) typewriter paper. Type your name and address in the upper left-hand corner of the first page of your manuscript. Leave wide margins—an inch on all sides.

After all these precautions, how does the unknown and unorthodox writer of short stories find an opening? By trying any vehicle that will carry him, and by continuing to write despite rebuffs and rejections. Ernest Hemingway finished his early stories while he was free-

lancing as a journalist in Paris, and they came into
print in the little magazines—*The Transatlantic Review*, *This Quarter*, and *transition*—for fees that were
minute or non-existent. Then in 1926 a friend urged
him to try the American market with a long, rugged
story about a prize fighter whom the gamblers were trying to bribe. After months of batting around and a
series of rejections of which I knew nothing, the story
came to me as the first reader for the *Atlantic*. At this
point and without modesty, I should like to quote Ray
Long, then the editor of Hearst's most popular magazine, *Cosmopolitan*:

W. C. Lengel was representing the Hearst group
of American magazines in Europe. One night, in
Paris, he went to a prize fight with some friends.
There he met a young chap named Hemingway,
Ernest Hemingway. He and Hemingway took to
each other from the start. During the evening the
new friend confided to Lengel that he'd written a
short story. Bill, always on the alert for new material,
asked him to send it around the next day. And in
due course the manuscript came across the sea to me,
and with it the most enthusiastic letter of praise that
I ever received from Lengel.

I read the story. It left me cold. Absolutely cold.
For the life of me I couldn't see why my associate
had got so excited about it. I rejected the story.

Next it went to *Scribner's*. Maxwell Perkins, one of

the most astute editors in the land, liked the story fairly well, but thought it should be cut down. Hemingway refused to do the cutting, and when some one else tackled the job it was found that the story, as edited, didn't make sense. The author, in writing it, had cut out every word that could be spared. Next it went to *The Saturday Evening Post*. And bounded back like a rubber ball. Next *Collier's*. Same result.

And then one night I picked up the *Atlantic Monthly* and started to read "Fifty Grand" just to see what they had done with it. They hadn't done a thing. But Ellery Sedgwick, editor of the *Atlantic*, had seen in the story what Bill Lengel had seen in it, and what the others, myself heading the list, had overlooked. And what I saw the minute I read the story in type.

Next day I wired Lengel to ask his friend, Hemingway, to forgive me for the stupidest blunder I'd ever made as an editor. For "Fifty Grand" was one of the best short stories that ever came to my hands. It was—and is—I think, the best prize-fight story I ever read.

This is a generous statement, but not, I think, too generous in its praise. And if one of Hemingway's best, this hard-boiled narrative of a fighter who hit below the belt, is tossed from pillar to post, to fetch up in the end in America's oldest literary monthly—if such things happen to a writer as promising as Hemingway,

**47**

surely it is not unreasonable to expect that the work of other beginners may have to spend some time on the road.

So, on the one hand, you have an army of young aspirants, each one sure that he has enough originality and skill to be published if only he can find the right editor, and, on the other hand, a corps of experienced editors with white space to fill and not enough good fiction to fill it. Is there any way that I can facilitate a break-through?

Many editors I have known prided themselves on discovering new talent, and the best of them, Maxwell Perkins, the editor of *Scribner's* books, and Harold Ross, the editor of *The New Yorker*, were in a class by themselves. I intend no cynicism when I say that it is easier to "discover" a new talent after it has begun to find its way into print than to spot it in a freshly-typed or long-traveled manuscript. Most magazines of mass circulation play safe; they take over the work of a new writer after watching his initial success in some smaller sheet, and in the transition, of course, they will pay him a higher fee—to keep him from reverting. Magazines which are less dependent on the newsstands can be more daring in their selection. Discovery, in short, is in inverse ratio to the size of the circulation, and this explains why *Harper's* and the *Atlantic, Encounter* and *The Partisan Review* are watched for new talent

and produce more of it year after year than all of the slicks put together.

More short story writers of ability came to our attention in the years 1945-50 than in any other period I can recall. Most were war veterans who had gone into the service fresh from college and whose writing had been deferred until their discharge. What they wrote about was the war, and many of their narratives were so good, so sure in detail, so charged with feeling that we set up a new department for them in the *Atlantic*. We called them *Atlantic* "Firsts", to signalize their first appearance in our columns, often, their first in print anywhere, and each December we gave sizable cash awards, in addition to their regular fees, to the two stories our staff regarded as the best in the twelvemonth. Some very able writers appeared as *Atlantic* "Firsts", including Thomas Heggen, Louis Auchincloss, Richard Yates, Peter Matthiessen, Cord Meyer, Jr., and James Jones, to name but six of some seventy, and our readers took such interest in their fresh, independent fiction that we have continued to encourage Firsts even though they are no longer dominated by the war.

As I read the work of these war veterans, I was impressed by their maturity and by the degree in which their work differed from the younger efforts that came to us during the depression. Social conscience and the

49

grievance of injustice were the yeast in so many stories of the 1930's—what Robert Frost called "The Tenderer-Than-Thou School"—and the central concern was so often for money or security. Dramatic action was sadly lacking; what happened was secondary to the mood of pity. In the post-war stories, action had returned, and it was violent; the threat was death, and the central concern was not success but survival. The mood was the mood of compassion, and there was an undisguised sympathy for at least one character, which was by no means the case in the '30s when the victims of injustice were so often presented as if they were charity cases whom one could pity but hardly like. Yet when Tom Heggen wrote his enormously popular war novel, *Mr. Roberts*—it was really a threading together of short stories, some of which first appeared in the *Atlantic*—there was not the slightest doubt that the author intended you to sympathize with his likable and luckless hero. So it was with the other stories; quietly but firmly they directed your sympathies toward one character, the joker in the company or the guy in the submarine who suffered from claustrophobia, the man in the next bed in the hospital who didn't make it, the girl your outfit rescued from the internment camp.

Somehow during the war and after, these young writers had read or read about Freud, Hemingway, Joyce, Kafka, Camus, Dylan Thomas and Robert Graves

and Eliot; they seemed to know more than their predecessors about what has been written, even though they
might not always be able to hit it right themselves.

Loneliness amounting to desolation was a war theme
which kept recurring, and I suppose we shall never
know how many marriages were broken by the long
intolerable separation. Husbands on foreign service running into years, wives whose husbands were prisoners or
reported missing—where could they turn for sympathy?
One of the first and finest stories on this touching subject was "Flesh and Blood", by Lawrence Critchell,
which won the O. Henry Award for 1945. A lieutenant
in the paratroops training for the invasion, young
Critchell—he was twenty-six—went to the very heart of
loneliness in this compassionate story of an American
officer and an English girl watching and finding each
other at a dreary movie.

The war did many things to fiction and particularly
to the short story. It brought back action, fast-moving
and violent, to what had become a static, introspective
medium; and it gave a far wider scope for compassion
and understanding, whether for the G. I. who was being
bitched at home or for the Italian war orphan adopted
by the bomber groups or for the wounded and broken
men who were to wind up in veterans hospitals. The
war gave an immense geographic spread to American
curiosity, and stories about Japan, the Philippines, India,

France, Germany, wherever our troops had been, took on a fresh new meaning. Those who had served overseas were inculcated with a sharper perception of what their home life should amount to, and there were many like Charles Gray, John Marquand's hero in *Point of No Return*, who on their return wished to escape from the ruts of their old jobs. Finally, to some young Southerners the war brought the realization that white supremacy and segregation were not a state of affairs sanctioned by the Constitution or approved by the world at large.

I remember a letter by a young Southerner in the Army which was published in *Time Magazine* towards the war's end and which I quote here because it expresses so vigorously the new idealism which I believe will leave its mark in southern fiction. He wrote:

> I never intend to work as hard again as I have worked during these three years in the Army. During the easiest days of training, the working day averaged better than ten hours, and about the only way we could recognize Sunday was by the absence of our Catholic colleagues. My next job will have to allow time for private, personal thinking, talking, reading and writing.
>
> I intend to live in the South again. There are the usual reasons for that decision—the ties of blood that never seem important until you've lived a long time away from home. Then, I don't think I've been really

warm since I left South Carolina in 1941; in Normandy I used to sleep in a puddle and dream of the long, bright days when good Southerners sit in the shade and watch the heat waves rise off the parched red earth and feel the sweat slowly run over their ribs.

I want to build a house, water a lawn, dig a can of beer out of my own refrigerator, get elected to a school board. I want to dig my roots into a community and regain the feeling I lost a long time ago.

Some day, when the weariness has passed, I'll want to get back into the old fight, of which this war is a military phase. I've come to believe that the important things, the essential freedoms, the democratic processes, are luxuries, not inalienable rights, and the price we must pay for them is high.

Early in the war a friend of mine named Al, who has one of the most pronounced Boston accents I have ever heard, was chewing the rag with his sergeant at the end of a hard day of boot training. The sergeant was from Brooklyn and his Brooklynese was a thing of beauty. "It's a funny damn war, Al," he said after listening to the Bostonian for some time, "and I suppose at the end of it, we'll all of us be talking the way you do." This was another by-product of throwing all Americans together. It helped to rub out local differences, especially in speech. The use of dialect in short stories had been fading for some time. When I was a

53

first reader, I suppose one story in every five came to us in dialect. They were written in Pennsylvania Dutch and in the quaint Elizabethan accents of the Kentucky mountaineer; they were written in Negro dialect, Yiddish dialect, in Irish brogue, in half Swedish, half Italian, half Armenian. But today stories in dialect are exceedingly rare, and I think this is better for the stories and better for us: it marks a milestone in our process of assimilation, for the stories which were written in dialect often were either broadly comic or broadly sentimental. Today the people of the bloodstreams I have mentioned wish to be heard in a language that is common to us all, and they deliberately avoid the mascara of dialect because they don't want their stories to be set apart or to be treated as something exotic or humorous or sentimental. In reading the stories of James Baldwin, one of the best of our younger writers and, incidentally, a Negro, notice how sparing he is of using the traditional Negro inflections of speech, and notice also the force and conviction which he is able to generate in the stories dealing with the troubles of his own people.

This is equally true of stories coming out of our metropolitan areas in which so many bloodstreams have been blended. In his novel, *The Last Hurrah*, Edwin O'Connor tells of an Irish politician who has outlived his power and who is about to meet his final,

crushing defeat. O'Connor is a master of dialogue; he served his apprenticeship in radio and television, and he has an exceptionally true ear for every nuance of conversation. In *The Last Hurrah* he has been careful to preserve the rhythm and the banter, the mischief and the affection of the Irish as they talk, but what they talk is American, not a brogue. There is a delicate trick to this; a very nice sense of balance is required to retain the rhythm of a local idiom without too much stress on an exclusively local vocabulary. But this can be done, and it is being done across the country today.

The war writers of whom I have been speaking, once the war books had been written, encountered unexpected difficulty in finding civilian themes of equal intensity. John Hersey, Herman Wouk, James Michener, and Norman Mailer are four who made the transition. Tom Heggen, the author of *Mr. Roberts*, and John Horne Burns, the author of that fine war novel, *The Gallery*, died before they could attempt the shift, and it is fair to say that James Jones, the author of *From Here to Eternity*, has been at his best only in fiction about army life.

The generation which was too young to go to war inherited as they came of age the inescapable worry of the atomic bomb and the lesser, but not negligible, worry of a world full of inequity, political and social

upheavals and private insecurity. Stories of lynching, stories of the persecution of Negro students, of Negro tenants in a housing development, of the prejudice against Negro laborers are decidedly on the increase, and this constitutes a problem to the editor who may be attempting to deal with these very same problems in his articles and who hesitates to stress them again in his fiction. Yet these old questions of justice, truth, and right are coming to us today with fresh emphasis not only from our own South, but from that highly talented trio of South African storytellers, Alan Paton, Nadine Gordimer, and Dan Jacobson. Nowhere in the British Commonwealth are there story writers to match them, and nowhere else in the Commonwealth are the passions of racial strife endured with such bitterness and stoicism.

One of the penalties of living in our time is that we and our children are so exposed to neurotic disturbances. We see them in the results of gang warfare, in the alcoholics and in the drug addicts, in the breakdown of gifted but too highly-strung students, and in the victims of manic depression. Short stories now venture into all of these areas of torment. It seems to me remarkable that no member of the Beat Generation has been able to cope with adolescence as perceptively as has J. D. Salinger. This is a field which he has made singularly his own, and he is emulated, he is used as

a model for young writers today as Hemingway was a generation earlier.

There are two traditional objectives open to any writer of fiction: to purge by pity or to entertain, and there is no need for a beginner to feel deprived of subject matter simply because his background and inclination do not equip him to write about disease or disaster. Presumably everyone would like to be revered as a literary landmark, but the writer like "Saki" (H. H. Munro), whose light fiction simply amuses readers, or like Katherine Mansfield, who added an extra luminosity to life, is not someone to be despised. In the summer of 1958 just before he went on a summer holiday with his wife and children, I persuaded Peter Ustinov to embark on a series of short stories for the *Atlantic*. He had never tried his hand at the short story before. He is one of the world's best mimics; he is a beautiful linguist who can improvise side-splitting monologues in at least five different languages. Through his acting and directing he has lived wherever good theater is produced except behind the Iron Curtain, and with these resources to draw on, he wrote stories which were cosmopolitan, full of surprising characterization and entertainment, and not without a touch of pity. He produced one a month during the eight months he was playing the lead in the road company of *Romanoff and Juliet*, and we published them in se-

quence, first in the magazine and then in book form under the title of his prize story, *Add A Dash of Pity*.

Humor and fantasy are both in short supply today, and an editor will be grateful to any newcomer who can supply stories of either ingredient. They are still to be found in our grim age, but the good ones are rare. P. G. Wodehouse has never budged an inch from his marvelous and inimitable frivolities. In Denmark, Isak Dinesen has produced her original and romantic Gothic Tales; in them she is working obliquely on ethical or psychological questions, but these are not thrown at your head, instead she conceals them in a surface treatment of the most skillful fantasy. In "The Secret Life of Walter Mitty," James Thurber is guying the little, hen-pecked husband anywhere. When you reread it see if you can detect where travesty ends and pathos begins. The apparent innocence of E. B. White's terrifying story "The Morning of the Day They Did It," which *The New Yorker* published when the bomb was first on our conscience, is a prime example of the swiftness and power with which fantasy can illuminate our real life. I can never forget that story.

On the other hand, you try to recall a really good story about Utopia. They may be laid in Heaven or on the lost continent of Atlantis or on Mars; whatever the destination, the purpose seems to be to show us a community which is run the way it should be, and

somehow the high seriousness emasculates the humor and the credibility. The best bit of Utopia I have ever read was "Moses" by Walter D. Edmonds, and that glimpse of the Heavenly Gates is redeemed by a man's love for a hound! Bear in mind that it takes a Milton— or someone not much less—to build a Paradise, and that even then his devils are likely to be his most "convincing" characters.

Thousands of what we call "the odd character story" find their way to the *Atlantic* each year, probably because the *Atlantic* showcase is one of the few remaining places which are open to them. The easy prescriptions of modern psychology are no doubt responsible for this increasing vogue. Villages whether in "decadent New England" or the monotonous Middle West supply the setting, and old maids are the favorite target. Everything about them is photographed in the prose— their dwellings, their keepsakes and their inhibitions. At the outset, the author parts the bun of gray hair and quietly unscrews the top of the old girl's knob; dexterously he runs his fingers through the gray matter; there are one or two stirrings of the heart, and then the gray matter is restored, the knob screwed back. The story begins with the old lady looking out of the window at the rain, and ends with the old lady looking out of the window at the rain. It is probably entitled "Rain." This is life.

I think women have had the most success with these odd characters, and there are two authors, Eudora Welty and Jessamyn West whose early work appeared in the *Atlantic* and whose books will well repay the study of any beginner. I remember a sequence of three stories which Miss Welty wrote for the *Atlantic* in the early forties. The first, "The Worn Path," the O. Henry prize-winner of its year, told of the resistance of an ancient little Negress whose shanty lay in the way of some urban development and who was determined not to surrender her foothold. This was followed by "Powerhouse," the character study of a Negro pianist, a band leader and of how he talked to and terrified his men as they played; and the third was "Why I Live at the P. O.," a kind of soliloquy by a zany little Southern spinster who lived as a recluse at a forgotten crossroad.

Much less successful are the stories—and they too are legion—which seek to glorify art. It seems like a natural wish fulfillment that a beginner should be tempted with the idea of writing a story telling of how fame, fortune, and a blonde come to an impecunious young man when his first play electrifies Broadway. But the trouble occurs when the author tries to make the reader share in the electrical effect of that play; the lines quoted from it are usually abysmal. The same charge can be pressed against the stories which are predicated on the success of a poet, a sculptor, or a

painter. Few of these ever really focus on the hard, discouraging years of apprenticeship or on the pitiful decline as a talent wears out. Instead the hero paints his picture or writes his epic as though it were the result of some divine visitation, and when he quotes from the epic you feel like holding your ears. Years before Joyce Cary undertook to write *The Horse's Mouth*, he studied painting; he knew how a painter works, and more important, how he sees and thinks. The authenticity of Gulley Jimson and his bohemian life which Cary created lies beyond the reach of most amateurs.

Art is miraculous, selfish, cruel—but most of all miraculous—and the stories about it have a fateful way of wandering off into the fantastic. They are prompted, I suspect, by a longing to escape from the prosaic, a longing to pay off old bills, have a sitter for the children, and spend the day writing, but, sad to relate, they are the least credible of any that we have to read.

The true art in the short story is the vitality that lives undimmed in the work of a really fine narrator. I put Ernest Hemingway as the best of our time, but there are others who follow close behind him. I think of those two exceptional Irish writers, Sean O'Faolain and Mary Lavin: O'Faolain who can recapture the past with such swift and telling detail, and Mary Lavin who writes of a drunken Irish fiddler, as in her story "At Sallygap," or of Irish spinsters or of a mother whose children have

61

left her for America, in a way to reach the heart. I think of Geoffrey Household, whose stories, whether placed in Chile, Roumania or Paris, are such masterpieces of suspense; of Stephen Vincent Benet, who wove together fantasy and history in a new blend as in his masterpiece "The Devil and Daniel Webster"; of Jessamyn West, who started writing when tuberculosis laid her low and whose first volume of stories for which I found the title, *Lead Her Like a Pigeon,* were about a quaint, tenacious lovable Quaker couple in Indiana; of Katherine Anne Porter, whose stories so often hark back to the Texas of her girlhood and whose people are so alive that they might be members of your own family; of Jesse Hill Ford, a newcomer from Tennessee, who captures the exhilaration of the revival, the medicine show, and the feuds which are still a part of the far backwoods. These are writers whose stories will serve as an incitement and as an example, and it may encourage the beginner if I add that five out of the eight I have mentioned were first published in the *Atlantic* at a time when they were unknown.

# IV

## 🌿 *THE ESSAY, DEAD OR ALIVE?*

THE ESSAY is as unpredictable as Cleopatra—and as attractive. It is a thing of moods, gay, introspective, as cool as Francis Bacon, as outraged as Elmer Davis on Senator McCarthy. Because we live in an anxious, didactic age, there are few who can maintain the poise and reflection required of an essayist; the more aggressive magazine article crowds the essay off the page, and there are those who pronounce it obsolete. And yet, in the past decade a Nobel Prize in Literature has been conferred on Bertrand Russell who writes essentially as an essayist. E. B. White in his essays has written more powerfully against atomic suicide than any novelist or article writer. Harry Golden's informal essays have made a disarming nationwide appeal for respect for Negro rights. Anne Morrow Lindbergh in her *Gift from the Sea* has pleaded the case of a woman's privacy as eloquently as Virginia Woolf defended her independence in *A Room of One's Own.* Edmund Wilson and Alfred

Kazin and Mary McCarthy in their critical essays have established a standard of literary judgment equal to the best to be found today in England. I don't see why we should throw in the sponge.

The essay is the prose of a mood, and the problem is how do you construct it? Well, some do it by walking for thought, as H. M. Tomlinson, the son of a London dock clerk, recaptured the great age of the sailing ships as he walked through the blitzed streets of Limehouse; or as W. H. Hudson, the sensitive naturalist, home again in England after years in the pampas, walked the streets of London with eyes closed, identifying each district solely by his sense of smell. Thoreau was a prodigious walker; as he walked he responded to what he saw on the shores of Walden Pond or along Cape Cod, and what he observed constantly stimulated his ceaseless rebellion against conformity. Many poets compose while on the move, and so do many essayists.

The essay is an act of personal disclosure, and every good essayist designs a style suited to the tone of his particular voice and capable of bare candor, teasing suggestion, half-veiled irony or proselytizing earnestness. You, the writer, are the central character in an essay; you may have an accomplice, but not a cast, and you are out to share an experience with your reader. You share your laughter, delight or pity, you share your deepening knowledge, awe and the quickening of the

spirit. And the spark of understanding, of mutual respect must pass between you and your reader or the paper is dead.

Style is the breath of the essay; it is the invitation and the enticement which makes friends out of strangers, prompting the reader to say, "Now there's a man I'd really like to know. It would be fun to talk with him." And then you do for a time, vicariously.

Listen for a moment to Henry Thoreau as he writes of Walden. The quotations are taken from his essay, "Where I Lived and What I Lived For." First, his account of the lake itself:

This small lake was of most value as a neighbor in the intervals of a gentle rain storm in August, when, both air and water being perfectly still, but the sky overcast, mid-afternoon had all the serenity of evening, and the woodthrush sang around and was heard from shore to shore. A lake like this is never smoother than at such a time; and the clear portion of the air above it being shallow and darkened by clouds, the water, full of light and reflections, became a lower heaven. . . . It is well to have some water in your neighborhood, to give buoyancy to and float the earth. One value even of the smallest well is that when you look into it you see that the earth is not continent but insular. This is as important as that it keeps butter cool.

And now listen to him again as he describes his reasons for being there:

I went to the woods because I wished to live deliberately, to front only the essential facts of life, and see if I could not learn what it had to teach, and not, when I came to die, discover that I had not lived. I did not wish to live what was not life, living is so dear; nor did I wish to practise resignation, unless it was quite necessary. I wanted to live deep and suck out all the marrow of life, to live so sturdily and Spartan-like as to put to rout all that was not life, to cut a broad swath and shave close, to drive life into a corner, and reduce it to its lowest terms, and if it proved to be mean, why then to get the whole and genuine meanness of it, and publish its meanness to the world; or if it were sublime, to know it by experience, and be able to give a true account of it in my next excursion.

It was Thoreau's genius to question the complacencies of life and to arouse his readers to a new awareness, and this he did in prose which flows with such clarity and directness that it looks easy. But try to simplify it further and you will discover that every word counts. Nothing can be altered without destroying some element of the scene that he has so carefully and accurately recorded.

Thoreau's closest friend was Emerson, and it was Mrs. Emerson, so I have been told, who each Sunday

night supplied the hermit with an apple pie and a loaf of homemade bread to help him through his week of privacy at Walden. Emerson's essays grew out of voluminous note-taking. He was forever poking things away in his notebooks, fragments as remarkable as this which follows:

> Eyes are bold as lions—roving, running, leaping, here and there, far and near. They speak all languages. They wait for no introduction; ask no leave of age or rank; they respect neither poverty nor riches, neither learning nor power nor virtue nor sex; but intrude, and come again, and go through and through you in a moment of time. What inundation of life and thought is discharged from one soul into another through them!

And then when he was pressed for a new paper, he would thread such things together just as he threaded this particular one into his essay, "The Conduct of Life." This passage embodies an essentially poetic idea, a leap of the mind beyond the normal limits of imagination and reflection. I quote it for its beauty—and as a warning to those who think that poetic prose is easy to come by. In fact, it is more often a distillation resulting from long, careful, subtle thought.

Much more attainable for most writers is the biographical essay. Max Beerbohm was a masterly ironist in this field, as you will see in his famous book, *Seven Men*, or equally in his penetrating portrait of the spent

and captive poet Swinburne, in the essay which he titled, "No. 2, The Pines."

A century earlier than Beerbohm, William Hazlitt, a cantankerous literary journalist with a finger in every pie in London, had a fine flair for writing about people. In 1824, Hazlitt published his paper "On Actors and Acting"; it was a most acute analysis of the profession. He wrote:

> Actors have been accused, as a profession, of being extravagant and dissipated . . . it is not to be wondered at. They live from hand to mouth: they plunge from want into luxury; they have no means of making money *breed*, and all professions that do not live by turning money into money, or have not a certainty of accumulating it in the end by parsimony, spend it. Uncertain of the future, they make sure of the present moment . . . An actor, to be a good one, must have a great spirit of enjoyment in himself, strong impulses, strong passions, and a strong sense of pleasure: for it is his business to imitate the passions, and to communicate pleasure to others. A man of genius is not a machine. The neglected actor may be excused if he drinks oblivion of his disappointments; the successful one, if he quaffs the applause of the world.

In those words of William Hazlitt's you have the balance and the contemplation of the nineteenth century.

Now listen as one of our contemporaries, Virginia Woolf, gives us her impression of William Hazlitt himself:

> Hazlitt's essays are emphatically himself. He has no reticence, and he has no shame. He tells us exactly what he thinks, and he tells us—the confidence is less seductive—exactly what he feels. As of all men he had the most intense consciousness of his own existence, since never a day passed without inflicting on him some pang of hate or of jealousy, some thrill of anger or of pleasure, we cannot read him for long without coming in contact with a very singular character—ill-conditioned yet high-minded; mean yet noble; intensely egotistical yet inspired by the most genuine passion for the rights and liberties of mankind.
>
> Soon, so thin is the veil of the essay as Hazlitt wore it, his very look comes before us. We see him as Coleridge saw him "brow-hanging, shoe-contemplative, strange." He comes shuffling into the room, he looks nobody straight in the face, he shakes hands with the fin of a fish; occasionally he darts a malignant glance from his corner. Yet now and again his face lit up with intellectual beauty, and his manner became radiant with sympathy and understanding. Soon, too, as we read on, we become familiar with the whole gamut of his grudges and grievances. He lived, one gathers, mostly at inns. No woman's form graced his board. He had quarrelled with all his old friends, save perhaps with Lamb. He was the object of malignant persecution—*Blackwood's* reviewers

called him "pimply Hazlitt," though his cheek was pale as alabaster. He had—no one would deny it—one of the finest minds, and he wrote indisputably the best prose style of his time. But what did that avail with women? Fine ladies have no respect for scholars, nor chambermaids either, so the growl and plaint of his grievances keeps breaking through, disturbing us, irritating us; and yet there is something so independent, subtle, fine, and enthusiastic about him —when he can forget himself he is so rapt in ardent speculation about other things—that dislike crumbles and turns to something much warmer and more complex.

Virginia Woolf, of course, never saw this man she was writing about, but note with what subtle perception and assurance she recalls him from the past.

In this age of high tension, we can expect to be badgered by the polemic writer though there are few today capable of the sharp logic and moral indignation of Tom Paine, or the artful horror contrived by Jonathan Swift in his "Modest Proposal."

Sydney Smith's essays denouncing the brutal poaching laws of the early nineteenth century were based on righteous fury, but Smith was a humorist, and no degree of rage could restrain him from calling the armed squire patrolling his coverts "a live armigerous spring gun." Smith was also a clergyman, and presumably no more in favor of sin than the average parson, but he saw small

good in The Society for the Suppression of Vice. The
Society was dabbling in the prevention of cruelty to
animals, and Smith observed that no attention was being paid to fishing, hunting, or boiling lobsters alive,
"all high-life cruelties." He goes on:

> The real thing which calls for the sympathies, and
> harrows up the soul, is to see a number of boisterous
> artisans baiting a bull, or a bear; not a savage hare, or
> a carniverous stag, but a poor, innocent, timid bear;
> not pursued by magistrates, and deputy lieutenants,
> and men of education, but by those who must neces-
> sarily seek their relaxation in noise and tumultuous
> merriment, by men whose feelings are blunted, and
> whose understanding is wholly devoid of refinement.

Whatever you think of bear-baiting, this is irony of a
fine order. Smith, incidentally, is an ancestor of the
modern article writer in one respect; he quotes and
documents to a remarkable degree. But his thesis is
always his own.

President Pusey of Harvard intended to compliment
E. B. White when, in conferring an honorary degree
upon one of the greatest of American essayists, he
called him "The Sidewalk Superintendent of Our
Time." Sydney Smith, denouncing the game laws in
England, and Henry Thoreau, jailed for non-payment
of poll tax, would have been outraged to hear themselves described as onlookers at the world. It was, in

71

fact, hardly a fair description of White, whose essays on the atomic future are informed with the sense of outrage. The role of Sidewalk Superintendent is the danger which now lies in wait for essayists, however, and White saw it as clearly as anybody. "Whenever I tell about spring," he writes, "or any delights which I experience, or the pleasant country, I think of a conversation I had with a friend in the city shortly before I left. 'I trust,' he said with an ugly leer, 'that you will spare the reading public your little adventures in contentment.' " But do not think for a moment that Mr. White is as casual as he appears in those words. He is a moralist whose hatred of brutality and abhorrence of war speaks for us all:

> Our own earth-bound life is schizophrenic. Half the time we feel blissfully wedded to the modern scene, in love with its every mood, amused by its every joke, imperturbable in the face of its threat, bent on enjoying it to the hilt. The other half of the time we are the fusspot moralist, suspicious of all progress, resentful of change, determined to right wrongs, correct injustices, and save the world, even if we have to blow it to pieces in the process. These two characters war incessantly in us, and probably in most men. First, one is on top, then the other—body and soul always ravaged by the internal slugging match.

That is more than a self-portrait; it is the reflection of every one of us at odds with an atomic age.

If fire like that has gone out of the essay today, it is, I suppose, because writers who are aroused feel that they must be heard quickly if they are to accomplish anything at all. They must hit out in the daily newspaper column or in a political weekly, and what they write seldom has the poise of the essay. We live, moreover, in a compartmented society. Hazlitt wrote on the theater, art, literature, politics, the education of women —or anything else that caught his eye. The man who scatters his shot like that today is likely to be brushed off as a fellow with no specialty. An author can hardly be blamed if he hesitates to risk being labelled a jack-of-all-trades and master of none.

With specialists writing for the journals of their trade and the politically acute preoccupied with the editorial pages, the essay is too often left to the amateur who doesn't know anything in particular and doesn't feel very strongly about it. There are exceptions, as I have said at the outset of this chapter. When Elmer Davis in his sturdy book, *But We Were Born Free,* stood up to combat the poisonous infection of McCarthyism, his essays were read and applauded the country over. When E. B. White celebrates the life on his small farm in Blue Hills, Maine, as he did in *One Man's Meat,* all of us read it with delight and envy. But too often the situation I have been describing results in meditations on the first crocus or the last leaf.

When such masterpieces remain unpublished, the word gets around that editors are not printing essays; editors meanwhile mutter among themselves that nobody is writing good essays any more. Both parties could be wrong if more good people will try.

# V

### 🌿 *SKIN AND BLEED*

AT THE TIME I was being groomed for the editorship of the *Atlantic*, one of our directors, Reginald Washburn, gave me friendly scrutiny. A wire manufacturer whose business had been successfully modernized by a team of industrial designers, he had a healthy respect for the magazine and an eager interest in keeping it young. When I would show him an advance copy of the upcoming issue, his invariable inquiry was: "Ted, what's the best Skin and Bleed you've got in it this time?" "Skin and Bleed" was his way of describing a true story of personal adventure for which the *Atlantic* has always had a special liking and most of which have come to us over the transom (i.e., uninvited) from young writers.

Skin and Bleed material has been an important ingredient in my make-up of the *Atlantic*, and the reason why so much more of it is coming to us today than in the 1930's is that now the country is sending overseas so many, many young people, most of them college gradu-

ates, in such a multiplicity of jobs. I think it began with the Marshall Plan; I remember talking at that time with a senior at Antioch College who had done his off-campus work in Walter Reuther's United Auto Workers Union and had just been enlisted in a group which was being sent over to work with the French unions. The outgoing movement, which is spurred by a spirit of dedication, has multiplied since then: It includes the juniors in our foreign service; engineers working on the water problem in Jordan or Ghana; metallurgists and representatives of our great oil companies; agriculturists contending against exhausted soil and the colonial curse of the single crop; young doctors responding as Albert Schweitzer and Tom Dooley did, to the call of under-developed nations; teachers and members of the Peace Corps, which is the most recent manifestation—men and women of this calibre are the Go-Outers of the 1960's. When they find themselves caught up in the stress of an unexpected and moving experience, they will write; they wish to share their experience with the family circle back home and when the truth in it is pressing enough, with the country at large.

Such is one origin of Skin and Bleed, and here is an illustration of how it comes to the *Atlantic*. There was a graduate of the Harvard Medical School who early in his Army service was sent out to the island of Bikini to help protect the Army and Navy personnel there against

radiation while the bomb tests were being made. He did his work with a Geiger counter, and as he scrambled over the rusty battlewagons which were serving as target, as he sampled the sand and sea water and listened to the salty talk of the ratings, he began to wonder what all this added up to. He had brought an empty looseleaf notebook along with him, and in it, during the tropical nights when he could not sleep, he began jotting down episodes and rumination. On the transport coming home, he continued to write of what he had done and of what he thought, and it was our good fortune that on his return to New England, Dr. David Bradley brought his notebook to us. When we published it under the title of *No Place to Hide*, first in the *Atlantic* and then as a book, young Dr. Bradley's exposition of the enormity of atomic destruction went home to the American people as no other account that had been written. It was the first thing he had ever published.

From India we hear from another young doctor, this one a graduate of the Harvard School of Public Health. Dr. Carl Taylor is the son of medical missionaries; he was born in India where he learned to speak Urdu as early as his English. Today he is working in close cooperation with the Hindu doctors combating the ancient diseases, malnutrition, and, most stubborn, the old superstitions which stand in the way of fresh knowledge in the tiny villages. His is an exciting job in one of the

77

most vulnerable of democracies, and though he had no training as a writer, he feels he must testify so that we shall better understand what is at stake.

The sea has a way of making people speak. John Masefield at fourteen serving in the British Merchant Marines got his first impetus from listening to the yarns of an old bosun; others not so poetically endowed are sometimes startled into writing.

A few years ago a transcontinental airliner bound for Bermuda with sixty-two passengers aboard was forced to make a crash landing in the Atlantic four hundred miles off Boston. The ship nearest to the SOS was a Boston Coast Guard cutter under the command of Captain Paul Cronk. He reached the plane while there was still daylight and before the seams had opened; aboard the plane, for the seas were high, the crew and passengers were almost helpless from seasickness and fear. The cutter stood up to the windward, laid an oil slick, called for volunteers and launched the long boat, and before darkness fell, every person in the perilous cabin had been ferried to safety. When Captain Cronk had returned to Boston and caught up on some sleep, we pressed him to tell us about this rescue on Station Charlie, which is the code name for that area of the Atlantic Ocean. He had never written anything but his log before, but now half dictating, half writing, he relived every hazard in that operation in a manuscript

that ran to 18,000 words. The details simply poured out, and when they were cut to the essentials we had a graphic, courageous sea story as stirring as anything in Hakluyt. Naturally, we called it *Rescue on Station Charlie.*

Landlubbers beyond counting have dreamed of the day when they could cut loose from home ties and sail away in a small craft of their own. Frank and Ann Davison were two who did. They had flown together as pilot and co-pilot, and Frank had managed an aerodrome in England until the war put a stop to civilian flying. Thereafter, their efforts to farm an island in Loch Lomond got them down, and in a mood of desperation in 1947, they invested their savings in the *Reliance*, a 70-foot fishing boat with "a jib-headed main and Bermudan mizzen"—and an engine Frank thought he could tinker back to life. They spent over £6000 on her and (still owing the last £2000) their plans were to sail across the Atlantic and on into the Caribbean with Ann writing articles for the yachting magazines to pay for their provisions. But there were delays, no "paying guests" were forthcoming, financial complications began to close in, and when at last they cut and ran for it, the *Reliance* did not live up to her name. "The Last Voyage" as Ann finally wrote it for the *Atlantic*, was a tragedy, for in the inevitable shipwreck, she alone survived.

79

Toward the close of his career I was admitted to the friendship of Dr. Wyman Richardson. A tall, broad-beamed Cape Codder with a magnificent torso that made him sit head and shoulder above us normal beings, Wyman had done the work of two men in his vast practice in Boston during the Second World War, and in the late forties as his strength began to ebb, he was obliged to limit his activity. In his retirement, he and his devoted wife Charlotte spent more and more time in their farmhouse on Nauset Marsh, with Nauset Beach and the rampant surf within sight and sound. This had been his be-all as a boy; he knew every mood of the sea and the marsh, and he never tired of watching the birds through his glasses or of trolling for the small striped bass, schools of which came in through the inlet on high tide. Here for his peace of mind—and to lay up something for Charlotte—he began to write, and when his manuscripts were finished, he brought them to me.

Dr. Richardson wrote mystery novels about the Cape which were as wooden as a saw-horse and which I could not help him to salvage, and, more as a pastime, he wrote informal short accounts of his life on the marsh, papers so observant, so beautifully economic in their expression, so alive that they were irresistible. We printed twelve of them in the *Atlantic*, and after his death they with other essays composed a book which

has sold steadily ever since. It is the distillation of Wyman's love for a particular time and place, written to preserve the fleeing hours for his family, and for strangers who could never know the Marsh so well. The chapter titles give you the range of his devotion: "Blue Crabbing," "Time Sense," "Bird Flight," "Tide," "Eel Grass and Depressions," "The March Doldrums," "Bird Language." Pause for a moment over "Do-Nothing Day," which is one of my favorites: It begins on a clear September morning in a mood of indolence. "Wy" plunks himself down on a low platform on the south side of the house with his bird glasses within reach, and there, perfectly still, he watches nature go about her business. A gray marsh hawk "hangs motionless on an updraft as he scans the grass for sign of mouse"; then the crows begin a racket as a very large red fox lopes out of the cedars . . . the focus shifts to a "stunning" pair of black swallowtail butterflies, the female "skittish," and shifts again to the antics of a large orange and black wasp who has succeeded "in killing (or drugging?) one of those big flying grasshoppers which are so common down here . . ." Is it strange that a man who could be so stilted in fiction could write with such easy precision in the essay? No, because when he wrote about Nauset Marsh, Wyman was reliving his happiest moments and was in command of every detail.

There are many opportunities for the beginner (Wy-

man began at fifty-one) in this panorama of nature writing, and there will be more in the future as more leisure is available, and as Americans travel further afield in search of recreation. Whenever I fly from coast to coast and look down into the dense coverage of the Appalachians or the Ozarks or venture at farsight into the untamed areas of Colorado or Wyoming or Arizona, I feel the stirring of pride in this great land and the desire to know more about our wild places. We are a mobile people and the urge to live for a time on a remote, uncultivated "frontier," be it an island off the Maine coast or as far away as Alaska, is deep in our heritage. Ninety years ago John Muir, a young naturalist, traveling the High Sierra with his burro, salt and a loaf of bread was the pioneer who, by what he said and wrote, saved for us the Giant Sequoias; today writers of his vision and power of observation are still in short supply.

Watch the skill and with what careful detail others make their approach. Sally Carrighar was reared in Ohio but came to her mature schooling in the Canadian woods and in the Far West. Her *One Day on Beetle Rock* tells with apparent tranquility but quickening tension of what transpired on a certain June 18th on a rock face in the High Sierra. I suppose that hundreds of hours of seeing—and recording—must have gone into this narrative which weaves together the lives of a

weasel and a lizard, of a grouse and a chickadee and a jay, of a black bear and a coyote, a deer mouse and a mule deer as they come and go, instinctively and in peril. Miss Carrighar is the unseen, accurate recorder.

The scheme, the matrix which will hold such details together in natural order, is very important. In his book, *Fire*, George Stewart sets out to trace the slow, terrible genesis of a forest fire in California from the moment a bolt of lightning makes the ignition in the dead leaves to the moment when the inferno is out of control; the timing will be the time required for the fire-fighters—and the wind—to extinguish the conflagration.

A canoe is a good matrix—anything can happen in a canoe. It may be a canoe trip leading to year-round isolation, such as that which James B. Rowlands made with his artist companion Henry B. Kane in *Cache Lake Country*, north of Hudson Bay. I remember what my friend David McCord said about that book: "The deep snows, the sun on the paddle blade, the smell of rotting pine, the feel of rain, the power of silence, the meaninglessness of measured time, the ever-changing balance of life against life—of these things Mr. Rowlands modestly writes at genuine first hand." Or it may be a present-day expedition in one of our more rugged national parks, such as Paul Brooks and his wife Ellen make each summer and write about afterwards in short compass for the *Atlantic*. They live off the country and the

streams and travel light, for the portages are long and rough—in one case, as long as the distance from the Battery in lower Manhattan to Times Square. Carrying your gear and the canoe on your shoulders that far can be galling. If it is to be true Skin and Bleed, such writing must not gloss over the blisters, the black flies and the unpredictable root that sprains the ankle. It needs humor just as much as the blessed relief to mind and body that comes with the evening meal at sunset; certainly a little sentiment but most of all a lively sense of participation.

# VI

## ❧ THE POET

THE *Atlantic* once printed an amusing satirical piece by Dylan Thomas, describing the proper dress, drink, habitat and conversation for poets. He caricatured all the types—the bucolic poet, the hearty proletarian poet, the languid aesthete with a poppy or a lily in his medieval hand. Of the writing of poetry, Thomas, who knew his trade as well as any man, observed merely, "It must be assumed that anyone wishing to take up poetry as a career has always known how to turn the stuff out when required."

If you can turn the stuff out, the real stuff, the kind that Kipling called "the magic," you will be published, although you probably will not get any money worth mentioning. You will be respected, although only by a small group of poetry lovers. You are beyond advice, because nobody, including poets, has ever produced a satisfactory explanation of how and where and from whom great poets learn their art.

But poets of this level have always been rare and are today, despite the fact that there are noticeably more fine poets about than there were thirty years ago. Aside from the first-class writers of poetry, I calculate that at least half the population of the United States at one time or another tries its hand at verse, and half of this verse is quite competent and even mildly charming, and all of it is submitted to the *Atlantic*.

No magazine complains of having verse submitted, provided it prints verse at all, for the only sure way to find and print new poets is to come on their work in a pile of manuscripts. But it is discouraging to read five hundred unpublishable poems for every good one and to consider the amount of time, effort, and hope that was put into the composition of these hopeless verses. It is also saddening to see the same errors repeated by three generations of poets.

Before I offer a list of awful warnings, I want to make one firm reservation. Whatever anybody lays down as a law about poetry is a generalization and can be successfully defied by a writer of sufficient power and ingenuity. It is a temptation to claim that the alternation of four- and three-foot lines is dangerous because it tends to fall into a tinkling, antique ballad style; but both Robert Frost and Robert Graves have used this type of metre with brilliant effect. The question before the would-be poet is, am I the equal of Mr. Frost and

Mr. Graves, or can I learn to be? And this can only be answered by experiment, first with verse and then with editors.

It takes a great deal of resolution, or possibly just plain brass, to write poetry. Why, offhand, should a druggist's assistant think anyone but himself would be interested in his reflections on an ancient jug? As it happened, he was right, and Keats's "Ode on a Grecian Urn" is still read, studied, and loved.

The modesty that didn't trouble Keats weighs on many lesser poets, however. Apparently it seems to the beginner that a verse attached in some way to an actual event is more respectable than one compounded out of his own imagination. This leads to the headline game, a very old diversion. The *New York Times* estimated that, following Lindbergh's flight, it received 10,000 poems celebrating the achievement, and this is no exaggeration, for when they were returned, they were all immediately readdressed to *The Atlantic Monthly*. We did almost as well with Rickenbacker and the seagull. Oddly, Sputniks and manned flights into space produced no such flood of topical verse; possibly the elements of accident, surprise, and individual effort were insufficiently present. The death of Dylan Thomas brought a tidal wave of lachrymose elegies, usually imitative of Thomas's own manner. The last drops of this inundation still roll in upon us.

In the case of comic verse, there is a further problem. The news item that inspires the poet to rhyme is usually so absurd in itself that the poem becomes an anticlimax. Several versifiers have reminded us that the Federal Income Tax Bureau does not allow a deduction for a silk hat eaten by a horse. None has contrived to better the plain statement. The extreme example of this kind of trouble was based on a news service story out of darkest Africa. I don't recall the actual name of the hero—call him Limpopo. The thing read: "Senator Limpopo Eaten by Constituents." Ogden Nash or Phyllis McGinley might have outdone this in verse, but our authors couldn't manage it.

If you cannot resist writing comic poetry about Senator Limpopo, bear in mind that the poem must go farther, and be funnier, than the fact.

Imitation is the curse of much of the poetry submitted to the *Atlantic*. Imitation is a hard thing to discuss, for the situation resembles that summed up in the definition of a statesman as "a dead politician." Every poet begins with the materials and techniques of his predecessors, and necessarily imitates. If Shakespeare had died before writing *Romeo and Juliet,* he would be remembered, if at all, as an imitator of Kit Marlowe. If Byron had quit writing with *English Bards and Scotch Reviewers,* he would be classified as the last of the 18th

Century wits instead of as one of the greatest of the Romantics.

The beginner must imitate earlier poets, as a child learns to talk by imitating his elders. When the poet has learned the elements and possibilities of the established poetic languages, he can go on to develop an idiom and a set of ideas peculiarly his own. If he does this so well that he arrives at greatness, he is no longer an imitator, even in his earliest work. Critics look back upon it with a kindly eye and refer to "the influence" of Skelton or Shelley or Eliot.

Imitation for its own sake is a common weakness of the hard-working aspirants who send us verse that we send straight back again. I mentioned the dirges for Dylan Thomas, composed in elaborate imitation of his own style. A great many people imitate Thomas these days, for his obvious tricks with language are fatally easy to ape. The delicate pattern of sound that underlies and indeed sometimes dictates Thomas's grammar is another matter, and evidently falls upon a good many deaf ears.

When Robert Graves published "The White Goddess," explaining his own attitude toward the writing of poetry, he inadvertently released upon us, and other publishers, a horde of poets who had determined to follow his example and keep a Muse. The mere fact that they thought they could keep one indicated that they

had misread Mr. Graves, who made it perfectly clear that he does nothing of the sort, Muses being uncontrollable. We suffered hundreds of manuscripts clanking with classical baggage and seething with portentous references to She or The Lady, by authors who simply did not understand the purpose or meaning of the fragments they had pillaged from Mr. Graves's argument.

When I first joined the *Atlantic*, the row about free verse raged merrily, with considerable attention being paid to Amy Lowell and her Imagists. Such pronounced adherence to a stylistic school is little heard of now, except for the Beatniks, who seem to have been so labelled by outsiders—not at all the same thing. We have "traditionalists" and "innovators," and each of these terms covers a vast, amorphous territory.

What used to be called free verse does continue to arrive, usually from high school students. I do not know whether this indicates that a large body of English teachers are still devoted to Amy Lowell, or merely that the young are too impatient to submit to the discipline of a formal metrical pattern. The ego, to be sure, has a much easier time of it in free verse. Here is a chance for elbowroom, freedom from restraint, and the temptation is to join one's voice to that "native" American chorus led by Walt Whitman, who cannot have foreseen what his followers would do. And free verse

does look easy—which may perhaps partially explain its vogue. I am inclined to think so when I unfold a page which has a family resemblance to Alice's version of the Mouse's tail—in effect something like this:

### THE ACCIDENT

Darkness. . . .
Chattering cold. . . .
The treacherous road
disappearing behind the curtain of fog.
The porch megaphones the sound of
voices, angry voices and a bitter laugh . . .
"—when you can behave like a gentleman!"
And a slamming door.
The motor pours out its driver's wrath . . .
Out of the fog, increasing cold,
come two beats with yellow eyes.
The cars leap at each other's throats.
Crash! Agony! Pools on the wet road . . .
Silence.
"Death Trap on North Main Street."

At its best, practiced by a masterly technician with a superb gift for grasping and conveying the overtones of commonplace events, free verse develops into the carefully calculated metrics of William Carlos Williams. At its worst, it is dull prose set up to look like what it is not, and deceives nobody but the author.

Real poets, says Santayana, create their own idiom.

This idiom is a thing of fashion, a fashion set by those ideas which are current at a particular time, as the ideas that produced the Commonwealth were converted by Milton into the foundation of *Paradise Lost*. Thirty years ago, the idea of evolution stirred popular imagination and awaited the coming of another Milton. He never arrived, but screeds about the cosmic process continue to do so, enriched by every extension of the scientific vocabulary. Unhappily, scientific terms frequently neither rhyme nor scan, and the poet who sprinkles his pages with "palæozoic protoplasms" and "thermonuclear holocausts" or refers, with romantic intent, to "all the tubules of my heart," displays more valor than discretion.

I do not wish to seem to advocate what used to be called poetic diction. The modern technical and scientific vocabulary began to be used, and successfully, in the thirties, by such poets as W. H. Auden and C. Day Lewis. It must be used if poetry is to be meaningful in the modern world, for when poetry does not represent the actualities of human experience it ceases to be poetry and degenerates into a word game. But the would-be poet who uses the latest popular scientific catch phrase to bring up to date a notion that has been tossed from one bard to another since Chaucer's day is cheating. The whole idea must be rethought in contemporary terms before the contemporary vocabulary

### November Impression

The dawn is opalescent,
The air so cool and slow,
The moon, a fainting crescent,
Doth of our sorrow know.

The east is undulating
With rosy tongues of flame,
Tall trees are crepitating
As though in silent pain.

The brooks are plashing softly,
A cock the welkin rings,
But our Tess lies so stilly,
And no Keats sings.

It need not be Keats. Any bird will do.

# VII

*THE INDISPENSABLES*

OUR COLLEGES AND UNIVERSITIES provide the stimulus under which members of the faculty both teach and write and under which a good deal of young writing is encouraged, and on every campus you will find at least one devoted and inspiring teacher of English composition. It gives me pleasure to call the roll of some of the best I have known: Dean LeBaron R. Briggs, Robert Hillyer and Archibald MacLeish at Harvard; Chauncey M. Tinker at Yale; Roy Cowden at Ann Arbor; Wallace Stegner at Stanford; Hudson Strode at the University of Alabama; Carroll Towle at the University of New Hampshire; John Ciardi at Rutgers; Robert M. Gay at Simmons College; and Edith Ronald Mirrielees at Stanford are just a few of a great company.

I never had the good fortune to meet the late William Strunk, Jr., who taught at Cornell and among whose abler pupils is the finest essayist of our time, E. B. White. Mr. Strunk summed up his teaching in a

96

Green began by asking Ronnie:

"Now then, Ronnie. What position did you take at the start?"

"I was on the outside at the start and I was glad I had that position, for I didn't run into the trouble that I would have run into if I had an inside lane position. So I ran down the straightway in about No. 8 position and it was a very comfortable position because no one was making a break at that early stage, and the whole field was bunched together in about 10 yards.

"In the second lap, the positions were somewhat the same, except that I didn't lose any ground, but a few men moved up from about 9th, 10th, 11th and 12th into closer position which put me into 11th position, but actually I had lost no ground on the leading runner so I wasn't worried. Now the second lap went about the same pace as the first, and I did notice a definite change in the pace when Murray Halberg had the pace taken away from him by the Australian boy, Merv Lincoln. He came over at the end of the second lap, and he took the pace from Halberg. He picked it up considerably and the whole field sort of moved with him, and then Halberg was in about third. I think he was straining badly even at that stage but we moved on that third quarter, and when we hit the bell the whole field had come as a group and bunched into a six-yard space, which was just fantastic. Twelve men all running together within 6 yards. I was in, I'd say, about 9th or 10th

99

position at this time. I had an inside position which wasn't too good, but my coach at school, Jumbo Elliott, always told me when in a box to just relax. So I relaxed, and next minute I saw Gunnar Nielsen of Denmark look back at me and he gave me the beck to move inside him."

Phil Green looked startled. This was new to him and everyone else in the studio.

"This fellow Nielsen is the man who ran against you when you broke the four-minute mile?"

"Yes, Gunnar Nielsen of Denmark."

"Yet he gave you the beck, he motioned for you to pass him?"

"He gave me the beck to move inside him, for which I thanked him from the bottom of my heart."

"He felt he was gone, of course?"

"He felt he had no chance at that stage."

"But he could have shut you out?"

"He could assist me or he could shut me out, as you say. Instead, he let me run inside him, and I took this very nice opportunity and moved inside him. Then I had a gap to move out on. This was at the 300-yard stage with Hewson now taking over the lead from Lincoln. I moved outside then, and we were in the back straight so I was losing no ground on the outside here because each man had to run the same length of the straight. I decided I would move up slowly and hit the bunch at 150 yards from home. I think I had planned this all along, before the Olympics. So I moved up slowly, still feeling very

100

good. Landy was ahead of me slightly and he was
really moving. He was working, you know. I got by
Landy pretty easy, and that put me in 4th position—
about 180 yards to go. When I saw Hewson in front
of me I said to myself, 'Gosh, this is Brian Hewson
—this is the guy that beat me at Lansdowne Road last
summer'—and I think I remember saying, 'There's
not going to be a repeat of Lansdowne Road.'
[Ronnie was beaten decisively by Hewson at Lansdowne Road.] So I really put the boot down, as we
say at home here, and I found that I was surging to
the front with very little difficulty. I hit the front,
and I knew I was going away from them at 50 yards
from the tape. I realized I had the race won, and I
sort of remember breaking out into a big smile, and
when I went through the tape I was so delighted I
threw my arms out in the air. I never felt so happy
in all my life."

How could anyone tell it better? And, of course, you
notice how precisely right are those two racy phrases
"he gave me the beck" and "so I really put the boot
down . . ."

The seven American astronauts who were chosen
for our space flights were known to be exceptional men;
what we did not know, until Colonel John Glenn spoke
publicly on his return, was with what natural grace and
precision he could express himself. From his address
before the joint meeting of Congress on February 26th,

I pick these characteristic utterances. The matter is, of course, spectacular, but see how his use of conversational idiom gives it the essential human touch:

Of his flight: "There seemed to be little sensation of speed although the craft was traveling at about five miles per second—a speed that I, too, find difficult to comprehend . . . we were able to make numerous outside observations. The view from that altitude defies description.

"I had listened earlier to Alan and Gus both describe this and was eagerly looking forward to it, and in their wildest use of adjectives they didn't describe what it's like even.

"Nor can I describe it.

"The horizon colors are brilliant and the sunsets are very spectacular. And it's hard to beat a day in which you're permitted the luxury of seeing four sunsets."

Of his anxiety about the heat shield as the capsule began to heat up for re-entry: "I could see flaming chunks go flying by the window, and I thought that if the heat shield was tearing apart it would be a bad day all around."

And at a later stage he made everyone smile when he said: "I think Caroline really cut us down to size and put us back in our proper position, though, when after being introduced, she looked up and said: 'Where's the monkey?' "

After such good muscular language as Colonel Glenn's, informed with humor and feeling, it is sad to think how much sawdust prose we have to submit to in speeches, telecasts and the ghost-written releases of business leaders and cabinet officers. The Eisenhower Administration is responsible for some rubbery phrases, the sooner forgotten the better, in my opinion: "as of now" (why not simply, "now") and "at all levels" are two of them, and then there is that word "massive" which can hardly be kept out of a press interview. Someone with a cousin on Madison Avenue came up with the words "massive retaliation," and it promptly became a pet lollipop for everyone in the Pentagon. The same grapevine produced the "agonizing reappraisal" and the "dynamic liberation" which members of the State Department under the late John Foster Dulles used for effect. President Kennedy's hardheaded wit comes rather refreshingly after such nonsense. "Khrushchev," remarked the President, "is a man who would trade an apple for an orchard."

In Chapter V, "An Approach to Style," which E. B. White wrote and appended to *The Elements of Style*, by his teacher, Mr. Strunk, Mr. White asks, "Who can confidently say what ignites a certain combination of words, causing them to explode in the mind?" Mr. White proceeds to give some suggestions and cautionary hints that "may help the beginner find his way to a

satisfactory style," and his recommendation No. 5 is so very pertinent that I should like to quote it here:

### 5. *Revise and rewrite*

Revising is part of writing. Few writers are so expert that they can produce what they are after on the first try. Quite often the writer will discover, on examining the completed work, that there are serious flaws in the arrangement of the material, calling for transpositions. When this is the case, he can save himself much labor and time by using scissors on his manuscript, cutting it to pieces and fitting the pieces together in a better order. If the work merely needs shortening, a pencil is the most useful tool; but if it needs rearranging, or stirring up, scissors should be brought into play. Do not be afraid to seize whatever you have written and cut it to ribbons; it can always be restored to its original condition in the morning, if that course seems best. Remember, it is no sign of weakness or defeat that your manuscript ends up in need of major surgery. This is a common occurrence in all writing, and among the best writers.

In your revision, you will be listening to the rhythm of your sentences; you will be looking for repetitions which occur when least expected, and more than anything else you will be questioning your choice of words. Henry James as a young man was a lover of adjectives; in his maturity he shifted his devotion to the adverbs; and when he revised his earlier novels, it was largely a

process of eliminating the adjectives and of inserting his favorite adverbs. But for those of us who are less finicky than Mr. James, the nouns and the verbs are what matter. "Write with nouns and verbs, not with adjectives and adverbs," advises Mr. White. "The adjective hasn't been built that can pull a weak or inaccurate noun out of a tight place." And so we go on racking our brains for better nouns and verbs than those we used in the first place.

We look for words in Roget's *Thesaurus* or in H. W. Fowler's *Modern English Usage* or in Henry Mencken's *The American Language,* three indispensable source books in which every writer ought to know his way about. Often when I have been prowling around in Roget, I have failed to find the exact synonym I thought I needed, but instead have come upon a word which was fresh and surprising and which set off a train of thought better than what I had. This holds true of the rhyming dictionary, which never helps with the poem you are working on, but sometimes sets off another one. The technical side of poetry is admirably summarized in Babette Deutsch's *Poetry Handbook, A Dictionary of Terms.*

Words are tools, and we never can have too many of them; it is all too easy to use those to which we are habituated. Not unless you make a constant effort to replenish and enrich your word-horde will your writing

hold for others the refreshing quality which you intend.

Like many other good things in life, the search for new words involves a certain danger. The word dredged from the depths of Roget and shoved into the text merely because it is odd, or because the author has taken too seriously injunctions against repetition, is likely to look like exactly what it is, a mixture of whimsy and cowardice. The border between originality and affectation is foggy. It should be travelled with some caution.

I have spoken earlier of the desirability of finding a friendly critic who will look at your work objectively and give you a verdict which is not sugared by affection. A good critic is indispensable, and it would surprise you to know how many well-established authors depend upon someone very close to them for the appraisal and criticism which they can get nowhere else.

Literary agents are, by the nature of their calling, practical critics of what will sell. They have to be if they are to prosper in their business. Like every good editor, they too are in constant search of new talent, but they cannot afford to take on a beginning writer until he has demonstrated his ability to turn out new material at a fairly steady rate—say at a minimum of six new pieces a year—and until they are convinced that what he is writing is worthy of being published. Of course they take chances. For their clients they play the part of an

editor, a critic, and at times a banker; they may advance him money—the late Harold Ober so befriended F. Scott Fitzgerald through the lean years—and most important, they brace the spirit and help a writer in his quest for new projects; by loyalty and affection they reinvigorate flagging energies.

Paraphrasing a remark of Woodrow Wilson's, I should say that in the years from twenty to thirty a writer should serve his apprenticeship, and that from thirty to fifty-five he should be capable of maximum production. Then somewhere between fifty-five and seventy his engines will begin to slow down—although this was not the case with Thomas Hardy nor is it with Robert Frost. The autumn of an author's career has both its ease and its discomforts. By now his mind has long been disciplined to operate in certain habitual hours of the day and operate it will, even if the light grows dim. Literature places a heavy strain on the eyes and many a man approaching his sapience has felt the need of more candlepower. Milton from necessity, Goethe from choice, both dictated their prose and verse after thirty; so did Henry James in his latter years; so did Robert Louis Stevenson in Samoa. Stevenson's daughter tells how he used to rise at dawn and, going off by himself, make note of the writing to be done that day. Then after breakfast he would dictate. Clarence Day fighting off the pain and captivity of arthritis was

still able to write within a limited period of each day those strenuous, nostalgic pages of *Life with Father*.

The most imperative of all indispensables I should say is privacy. When Leonid Leonov, the Russian novelist, visited me in Boston as one of a delegation of Soviet writers, I had the satisfaction of paying him in dollars for an episode from his new novel which I wished to print in the *Atlantic*. The day after he received the check, he asked to be taken to the best radio shop in Boston, and in the Radio Shack he purchased and had wrapped up for the long trip home a very fine instrument indeed.

"Is this to be a gift?" I asked.

"No," he replied, "all my life I have written against music, and now I want the best that can be had." What he meant was that in the overcrowded living conditions of Moscow, he, as a struggling writer, had had to do his work in the midst of household turmoil and interruptions, but by playing the radio as he wrote he raised a wall of music shutting him in with his thoughts. And now that he was famous and wealthy and had privacy, he still liked to do his writing with music filling the room, and he wanted the best.

The truth is that writing is *the* most solitary of occupations. Writers who live in the city hire a furnished room at a distance from their apartment, if they can afford it, to hide away from their family when they wish

to work. Those in the country will convert a small barn or a tool shed for their purpose.

Sarah Orne Jewett did her best writing in a deserted country schoolhouse. At Quarry Farm, Mark Twain had "a little room of windows" built on a hillside, and there he stayed three-quarters of the day writing. He never ate luncheon, and his family rarely dared to venture within gunshot, for Mark had a hot temper and hated to be disturbed.

Given time, ambition, something to say, and all the tools of the trade at hand, writing is still not easy. For it is always, in the end, not a trade at all, but an art, and therefore requires of the artist nothing less than the absolute best he can do.

In the Preface to his novel, *The Nigger of the Narcissus,* Joseph Conrad wrote:

> . . . the aim of art . . . is not in the clear logic of a triumphant conclusion; it is not in the unveiling of one of those heartless secrets which are called the Laws of Nature. It is not less great, but only more difficult.
>
> To arrest, for the space of a breath, the hands busy about the work of the earth, and compel men entranced by the sight of distant goals to glance for a moment at the surrounding vision of form and color, of sunshine and shadows; to make them pause for a look, for a sigh, for a smile—such is the aim,

difficult and evanescent, and reserved only for a very few to achieve. But sometimes, by the deserving and the fortunate, even that task is accomplished. And when it is accomplished—behold!—all the truth of life is there: a moment of vision, a sigh, a smile—and the return to an eternal rest.

# VIII

## ❧ THE BOOK AND THE EDITOR

I OPENED this book with the beginning writer in mind and have explored some of the more accessible ways in which he might break into print. I have spoken of the changes in reading habits and in editing that have occurred since the 1930's, and I have scrutinized the article, the essay, the short story, and verse as we find them today in American periodicals. In all this I have been advising as a magazine editor. Now in the space remaining I want to look into the opportunities and the problems which confront the writer of a book. It has never been easy for an unestablished author to get a hearing; I think it harder today to do so than at any time in this century.

The ratio between the book manuscripts written and those which are published is, generally speaking, fifty to one—fifty attempts to one acceptance. I am glad to say that these odds neither deter writers from writing nor editors from reading manuscripts submitted to them. As

111

R. L. Duffus said in his *Books: Their Place in a Democracy*:

> It would be a cause for rejoicing if a million Americans were trying to write books, first, because people who try to write can be counted on to read; second, because out of a million manuscripts we could expect to sort out more good books than we do out of a fifth or a tenth or a twentieth of that number.

The approach to publishing is complicated at the outset by a sense of mystery: A manuscript is submitted, and immediately there ensues a silence which grows the more mysterious as it is prolonged, and which is seldom satisfactorily explained by the letters of decision that in forty-nine cases out of fifty must be of polite rejection. Most such letters are of necessity evasive: The editor cannot analyze failure in detail and he must not raise false hopes if in his judgment the manuscript is hopeless. Only when he goes into detail is it a sign that he and his staff have been more than casually interested.

The business of publishing is dependent upon the question of taste, which leads to anarchy and misunderstanding. It is just as natural for a writer to believe in what he has written as it is for a publisher to rely upon the tests of his experience, and this personal equation is further complicated when a literary agent is involved, for the agent will almost invariably take sides with his

client, the author. I have been long enough in publishing to have no mere pontifical regard for editors, and I should like—if I am able— to explain away some of the mystery and the antagonism that surround the handling of book manuscripts.

The sincerity of a writer is taken for granted; that of a publisher is not infrequently questioned. "I know you editors never read all of your manuscripts," a letter will say; or "I am sending you my story even though I have been told you never accept unsolicited material," writes another; or, more fantastic still, "I am submitting my book with faint hope, since I am aware of your prejudice against Catholic writers." There was a woman who pasted together the latter pages of her manuscript in order to determine whether or not every word of her novel had been read. There was a man who wrote me angrily declaring that his repeated rejections could only be explained by the fact that he was on the publishers' "black list"—and threatening to sue me if he was!

It should be accepted without question that a publisher steadfastly examines the chance manuscripts that come his way. Unsolicited material is generally disposed of rather more rapidly than that which has been solicited. It is only natural that a cleanly typed manuscript will inspire more hope than one which is dog-eared or stained with travel, and inky with over-writing. But *all* the manuscripts will be read. Don't think that there is

113

a "black list" of rejected authors which circulates in editorial circles: A publisher survives in a competition which is strenuous and cutthroat, and it gives him solid joy to discover and sell a book which he suspects or knows has been turned down by competitors. George Meredith, when he was a manuscript reader in London, turned down the first novels of Thomas Hardy, but the point to remember is that Hardy promptly found another publisher. James Joyce had a fearful time getting his first collection of stories, *Dubliners*, into print. The manuscript, which Joyce had begun to write in 1904, was completed in 1905, but two publishers because of Edwardian squeamishness broke contracts with the author to avoid the risk of sponsoring the book. In 1912, Joyce thought he would publish the book himself and went to Dublin to buy the sheets, but the printer not only refused to sell them to him; he destroyed them and broke up the type. *Dubliners* was finally published in 1914—ten years after the author had begun to write it.

Erich Maria Remarque's *All Quiet on the Western Front* went on to sell half a million copies after being refused by the first American publisher to whom it was offered. And the press of which I was in charge has given two five-thousand-dollar prizes to book manuscripts which we later learned had languished unrewarded for months in rival houses.

These are but conspicuous examples of what is happening daily in the business of publishing. And, keen though the pleasure may be of scoring a success off an opponent, there is, I promise you, a still greater satisfaction that comes occasionally to a publisher—the satisfaction of detecting hidden talent and then, by the exercise of the editor's persuasion and the author's ability, of encouraging this talent to its fullest expression. I remember Kipling's devotion to F. N. Doubleday, his American editor, who personally and professionally had encouraged him from the first; how Edward Garnett, a reader for a London publisher, helped to develop the inexperienced Conrad; what Maxwell Perkins, the editor of Scribner's, meant to the lumbering, powerful Tom Wolfe in the final shaping of *Look Homeward, Angel*; and the unfailing support one of my own associates, Seymour Lawrence, gave to Katherine Anne Porter in the protracted finishing of her impressive, big novel, *Ship of Fools*. Between these authors and editors the business of publishing was no mere matter of contracts and royalty statements. Theirs was a friendship founded on mutual respect, and strengthened by the give-and-take, the criticism and appraisal, which every writer needs. This is publishing at its best.

I have said that all manuscripts that come to a publishing house are examined, and so they are. In the editorial department of book publishing houses as with

magazines, they are first read, not by the editor-in-chief, but by a professional manuscript reader, a person whose identity is usually concealed behind that cryptic signature, "The Editors." Do not suppose, however, that this anonymity is a cloak for inexperience: A trustworthy reader is as indispensable to a publishing house as is a magnetic and mature editor. Willa Cather was a manuscript reader; Frank Swinnerton, Blanche Knopf and Lillian Hellman were three of the famous readers I looked up to when I broke in. Because most of you will try your cases before such judges as these, it might be fitting for me to give you Mr. Swinnerton's qualification of this superior court of letters:

The professional reader's task is very different from that of a reviewer, and much less simple. The publisher's reader must have no vagaries. His prejudices must all be sunk when he takes up a manuscript. He must combine enthusiasm with calm; caution with boldness. He must be patient, wary, shrewd; he must know something upon every subject; he must be acquainted with all literatures, and, preferably, with several languages. He must understand the book trade, must have a very easy familiarity with the work of all living authors . . . He is expected to mark down a bestseller at sight, and to distinguish between work that is immature through excess of genius and work that is crude through congenital incapacity. Taste, experience, and a subtle enjoyment of drudgery for the sake of its

occasional rewards (purely spiritual, since he rarely experiences gratitude) go to form the publisher's reader. Such readers have known the best when they saw it—so much is easy to the real critic. They have known, or thought they knew, a best-seller when they saw it—that is not so easy, even to the born publisher. And they have known and backed with their recommendation and encouragement every variety of literary promise: and this is the greatest service which they could possibly render either to the publisher or to the cause of modern literature. Such service could only be given by minds trained, patient, and extraordinarily perceptive. It calls for a special sort of courage, possessed by few men.

It is an editor's duty to cut when necessary, to call forward and to inspire when a writer's initiative is low, and in time of stress to suggest that very title which will give a fillip to the whole. Remember Michelangelo's fine saying, "The more the marble wastes, the more the statue grows." Remember the lady who complimented a bishop on his sermon, but added that she thought it was a bit too long. "Madam, I did not have time to make it shorter." We are all of us addicted to long-windedness, and it usually takes our wives or some other patient first reader to tell us so. I have known of autobiographical notes which ran to nearly eight hundred thousand words, but which were breathed on by a capable editor and came out a readable book of one-eighth

the size; I have known where small omissions amounting in all to but three thousand words were a means of shifting sentimentality into true feeling. Have patience with the editor if he wants you to leave out parts of your manuscript. He is probably right.

Or let us suppose that a good title is missing. I recall a short manuscript submitted, then sent back for revision; resubmitted and returned for still other alterations. On its third call it was accepted. All during this process it was known as "The Dago Pig Episode," for that was what the author, Ellis Parker Butler, called it. But when it was published it was" Pigs Is Pigs," and the editor had done the christening!

Nothing tempts an editor more than the possibility of revision. Again and again I have come upon book manuscripts, long, crude, ungainly, or extravagant manuscripts which on the surface deserve rejection, yet within which are flashes of material whose promise gleams through the duller verbiage. Is it plausible to believe that in a guided revision the author could sustain such quality? If the whole thing could be taken to pieces, reorganized and rewritten would we have a book worth printing? ("Had we but world enough and time . . . !") In such cases, I should much prefer to write a letter of frank criticism rather than of polite evasion were it not that the first course may end in a disappointing failure. If a manuscript has interested me, I have

probably taken notes about it, and if these point to a rejection, they will also show where and why the story has gone off the track. Should these notes be embodied in the letter of rejection? What decides me is the amount of revision which I think may be necessary, for I know that the law of averages works against large-scale rewrites—they almost never come off.

And there is another factor: The time and industry which are represented in the writer's work, and out of respect for which something more than a noncommittal reply is due. In the face of such circumstances, I think the rejection should be as specific as the interest warrants. If the editor holds little hope for the manuscript, he need only mention the main objections to it; if, on the other hand, he believes that it might perhaps be salvaged, he should be specific even to chapter and page. The writer must understand that he is undertaking a revision with no definite assurance of acceptance, yet even so he will often be willing to take the gamble.

In reading manuscripts I watch for anachronisms and phrasing not well fitted to the substance; technical misstatements and those repetitions of favorite words which have a way of escaping even the most scrupulous writers. In addition, I am on the lookout for these larger inconsistencies:

1. Episodes which are incredible. Often an author will defend such incidents by declaring that they ac-

tually happened. But that is not the point; they must look real *in print*. Episodes that stretch the reader's credulity to the breaking point can sometimes be mended by omitting extravagant details, sometimes omitted entirely.

2. Loose ends. Many an author has the habit of turning away from his episodes before their conclusions are fully understood by the reader. The editor should accordingly indicate those paragraphs or sections which need amplifying.

3. Identification of characters. In long books having a large cast, when the author reintroduces the names of people whom the reader may have forgotten since first they were mentioned, a reminder of who they are must be inserted.

4. The threat of libel. Through the mouths of his characters the author may say some harsh and damaging things about living people and institutions. Will these comments stand the test of law? Libel suits are seldom worth the notoriety and expense involved.

5. Slang and colloquialisms. They must be timely. Whether they appear in the author's introspection or in the characters' dialogue, they must not be used in advance of their actual currency. No Victorian ever said, "This is a lousy play!"

6. Improprieties. In much modern fiction there may be lurid passages, passages of over-determined brutality, passages whose sexuality or plain animal bestiality are meant to hit the reader between the eyes. Shall they be preserved as they stand, or should they be modified? An editor is apt to follow his instinct, knowing full well that in a question of taste such as this the author is not only consulted but generally has the last word.

7. Manuscripts too long for their own good. In which case the extraneous flesh should be cut away, more often in paragraphs than in pages and always so as not to cut main arteries. It has to be a very great artist like Tolstoy to sustain a novel as long as *War and Peace*. We can all think of contemporary novels which rival Tolstoy only in their length and which surely would have been better reading had they been cut by a third.

Again, I am not implying that editors are infallible. I know too many cases of mistaken judgment ever to have that kind of stiff neck. My hope is that where one publisher misses the promise in a manuscript, another will be almost sure to detect it. And finally, I know that the literary agent, who is so much more of a factor in publishing today than ever in the past, can give new writers a direction that is invaluable. I have asked one of the best in the business to sum up for me the nature of his work. Here is his reply:

My ambition is to arrange an author's outlets so that he can do the amount of work he can do best with the highest return to him. In some instances, an author might do his best work if he turns out a million or more words a year, and another if he did only eight to twelve finely polished short stories in the same time.

My difficulties usually occur where two people (editor and author, or publisher and author) in bargaining misunderstand each other. I try to make each of them believe I was at fault whether I was or not. They then are united in being annoyed with me and forget their differences. Later they forgive me.

I have no opinion as to how many people can be handled by any one agent. My rule is to stop handling anybody pronto if I find the author's work is being negotiated perfunctorily.

It depends upon the writer how much in the way of ideas or criticism you can give him. I invariably insist that a writer understand that I offer only a perspective on his work, that if what I say does not sell itself to him, I'm wrong 100 per cent. To suggest books, articles, etc. is a function that is valuable, and the more an agent can develop this the better for him. The publishers like this also; they feel it an extension of their editorial department. This has been in a measure responsible for the ever-increasing good will between publishers and agents.

One more point, that of shifting authors from house to house. Our policy has been never, if possible, to allow only the matter of larger advances and royalty rates to affect such changes. A publisher and author

should continue their partnership so long as mutual trust and enthusiasm remain. But to keep a truly discontented author with a publisher brings about no more good than keeping a basically unhappy marriage alive simply because it's not good form to separate or divorce.

This last point involves the ethics of what in expansive moments publishers like to call their profession; I should like to discuss it with candor in the chapter that follows.

# IX

## A YOUNG WRITER IN THE ATOMIC AGE

A YOUNG WRITER in the atomic age must do his work under an atmospheric pressure from which there is no escape. On the bright side there is the incentive of writing for an eager and enlarging readership. Many factors have contributed to the revival of interest in books, chief among them the undergraduates, nearly a third of whom are studying under some form of student aid or scholarship and who must have inexpensive books; it is they who have sparked the demand for the better paperbacks. In 1961 the American public purchased over 380 million copies of paperbound books, and while the majority of them were westerns, detective stories, and sex teasers, an increasing minority running well up in the millions were reprints of the *best* writing that has been published.

On the dark side, the beginning author must write

124

against the fatalism induced by his knowledge of the bomb and of an arms race in weapons which, were they triggered, could blot out half of mankind. The threat of extinction is throttling to the self-confidence without which no author can finish what he has begun. Finally, the young writer must set his standards in the face of a vulgarization which was predicted by Ortega y Gasset in his famous book, *The Revolt of the Masses*, and which has contaminated our books, many of our magazines, and far too many of our television programs.

The living wage we pay our young authors is a disgrace to a nation which prides itself on being literate and wealthy. Suppose we take the case of a writer who has just published his first novel. His book has been long in mind and the actual writing of it occupied the greater part of a year; he and the editor have been over every paragraph, tightening, polishing, and eliminating the purple passages and the unessentials. This story of some 90,000 words, the length of the average novel, makes its appearance to the applause of the author's home town; there is an autographing party, two brief interviews on television, some fairly encouraging reviews, and as much advertising as $1,000 will pay for. The author cherishes but keeps to himself the hope that the success of this novel will establish him securely as a freelance. The publisher who has printed 4,000 copies of it in the first edition knows that he will not even reach the break-

even point until all the 4,000 are sold. His profit will come in the later editions—if any.

But the hard truth is that most first novels do not sell as many as 4,000 copies in the United States. Of the four first novels which appeared under the Atlantic-Little, Brown imprint in 1961, one—the success—went to a sale of 8,542; one went to 5,200, and the remaining two, as the unsold copies were returned by the book-sellers, dwindled to 3,000 copies or less. Those four deserved a better fate; they were not crude or clumsily written, and they did hold the vivacity one ought to look for in young books. I blame their failure partly on the high price of all American books in cloth, partly on the difficulty of promoting an unknown, but chiefly on the fact that American readers are so unadventurous. A man will not hesitate to spend $14.00 for a pair of seats to a new show, but he will shy away from a $4.50 novel by a writer he never heard of.

I wish this were not so, for see what happens: the young author whose hopes I have referred to finds that at the end of eight months' sale he has coming to him a royalty check of $1,831.60. Since he is thirty, married and the father of two children, the inexorable arithmetic of the royalty statement shows that he must continue to support himself by his teaching or journalism or whatever, and write his fiction on the side.

What seems hard usage for a beginning novelist is even harder for the young poet. The sale of a new book of verse in the United States falls between 600 and 1,000 copies with an earning power for the author of from $300 to $500. Over the past decade the American poets who have been able to support themselves *by writing poetry* can be counted on the fingers of two hands. I shall list four that I know of to start you guessing: Robert Frost, Carl Sandburg, Phyllis McGinley, and Ogden Nash. Most of our promising young poets are obliged to teach. This is good for the universities, but is likely to keep the poet under wraps. Does it not seem preposterous that the several hundred thousand Americans who aspire to write verse should spend so little of their thought and cash on the living poets who really can?

I deplore the public's apathy toward modern poetry, their coolness toward the essay, and most of all their temptation to read only the books which the Joneses are reading (see the current list of bestsellers) instead of picking and choosing according to their personal bent as the British do. But I am old enough to realize that these conditions are not likely to change overnight. A beginning author must accept them as part of the odds against him, just as he must accept the fact that the lazy man's vaudeville, which is television, has appropriated the reading time of many middle-agers, and that

the long-playing records compete with books on a fairly even basis for the undergraduates' dollar.

The beginning author will write because he must, because the impulse is so compelling that he cannot do otherwise. He will be buoyed up as are all artists, spasmodically, by the conviction that he has something worth saying, and that if he can only say it as eloquently as he hears and sees it in his mind, it will be worth reading. Not every year perhaps, but at regular intervals, he sees that authors do crash through all barriers of indifference with books which are feasted on by Americans of all ages, books whose sales still climb up beyond the half-million mark: *By Love Possessed* by James Gould Cozzens, a novel five years in composition and worth waiting for; *Dr. Zhivago*, by Boris Pasternak; *Ship of Fools*, Katherine Anne Porter's big novel which holds the beauty and distillation of twenty years' work. The happy welcome accorded *The Love Letters of Phyllis McGinley*, a volume of enticing verse which went through edition after edition, was a boon to all young poets, for it showed that the thing could be done despite the odds.

There are a number of difficult decisions which the book-committed writer must figure out for himself, and I suppose the most important is when and where shall he work: as far away from the telephone and other do-

mestic noises as he can get, in the cellar or under the eaves or out in the woodshed, and at a time which must be adjusted to his more gainful employment.

The lucky ones, or perhaps I should say the wise ones, find a paying job which does not exhaust the mind and the doing of which may help to color and enrich the writing they do when they are free. Robert Frost was a schoolteacher, he worked as a mill hand, and he farmed, but always with the reservation which he held to most tenaciously, that his primary job was to write poetry. In his apprenticeship as a sports writer, Ring Lardner reported some fourteen hundred baseball games and innumerable prize fights, and, as with Damon Runyon, journalism developed his true ear for reproducing the tough talk of those trades. Edwin O'Connor, the author of *The Last Hurrah* (and more recently of the Pulitzer Prize-winning novel, *The Edge of Sadness*), came to his novels by way of radio and television studios, and in the process, he developed an infallible ear for dialogue. When he was a young bachelor, Richard Bissell served as a riverboat pilot on the Monongahela and the Mississippi, and after he married and settled down, he worked in his father's shirt factory. From the initial experience came the setting for his first novel, *A Stretch on the River*, and from the second his more popular books, *7½ Cents* and his musical comedy *The Pajama Game*. Sinclair Lewis tapping out his first novels by night after

129

spending his day as a publicity man for a New York publisher; Joseph Conrad coming back from the sea in his mid-thirties to write with such painful precision—300 words a day was about his limit—in a language which he still spoke with a heavy Polish accent; John Galsworthy rebelling against the career at the Bar for which he had been trained; Somerset Maugham escaping from his internship at St. Thomas's Hospital to write a play —each approach is different and in each there is the compromise with necessity.

It takes perseverance and courage, and all the free time a writer can manage. And it takes hope, for to many the ultimate recognition comes belatedly. In his reminiscences, *Far Off Things*, Arthur Machen wrote:

No; the only course is to go on stumbling and struggling and blundering like a man lost in a dense thicket on a dark night; a thicket, I say, of rebounding boughs that punish with the sting of a whip-lash, of thorns that most savagely lacerate the flesh . . . Such is the obscure wood of the literary life; such, at least, it was to me. You struggle to find your way; but again and again you ask yourself whether, for you, there is any way. You think you have hit upon the lucky track at last . . . How old was glorious Cervantes, now serene for ever amongst the immortals, when he found his way to that village of La Mancha? Fifty, I think, or almost fifty. And he had been striving for years to write plays, and

130

poetry, and short stories of passion and sentiment; and it was only the roar of applause that thundered up from the world when the Knight and the Squire were seen riding over the hill that convinced Cervantes that at last he had discovered his true path; if indeed he ever were convinced in his heart of the magnitude and majesty of the achievement of *Don Quixote.*

The hurt of long rejection sounds through those words of the Welshman who, like the great Spaniard he admired, was well past middle life before he found his acceptance. Cervantes was a veteran of many campaigns, and like many veterans, he was often in debt and sometimes in jail; indeed, the legend has it that much of *Don Quixote* was composed while he was dwelling within the security of prison walls.

In the opening pages of A. E. Housman's *Last Poems* this note appears: "I can no longer expect to be revisited by the continuous excitement under which in the early months of 1895 I wrote the greater part of my other book." His "other book" was, of course, that little classic, *A Shropshire Lad.* Every writer of high or low degree has responded to this excitement, and not infrequently it was the driving force of his very best work. Thus the testimony of a young demobilized German veteran named Erich Maria Remarque, who tried teaching school while his wounds were healing and then

gravitated into the automobile industry, and thence into publishing:

In the spring of 1928, I was employed as "picture editor" of a periodical. The evenings I devoted to a variety of things. Thus for instance I made a number of attempts to write a play, but I never was very successful in that. I suffered from rather violent attacks of despair. When attempting to overcome these attacks, it happened that gradually, with full consciousness and systematically, I began to look for the cause of my depressions; just in consequence of this intentional analysis, my mind reverted to my experiences during the war. I was able to observe quite similar phenomena in many acquaintances and friends. We all were—and are often to the present day—the victims of restlessness; we lack a final object, at times we are supersensitive, at times indifferent, but over and above all we are bereft of any joy. The shadows of the war oppressed us and particularly so when we did not think of it at all. On the very day on which these ideas swept over me, I began to write, and this without a lengthy reflection. This was continued for six weeks, every evening when I returned from the office, and by that time the book—*All Quiet on the Western Front*—had been completed. . . . To understand a situation is the best means of escaping it. This idea was also expressed and confirmed in many letters written by men of my own age. They all sensed the book not as a pessimistic product but as a relief; the conditions under which they had suffered as long as they had not been brought to their consciousness had

lost their power over them, simply because they had been given here a clear-cut expression.

Thus under emotional stress and out of a past that had depleted him, Remarque wrote his full-length powerful novel in six weeks. I think this stands as a record. I have known dramatists to complete the first draft of a play in that time or less, but I do not know of any other case in which a fine novel was projected so swiftly. Despite the international success of *All Quiet on the Western Front*, Remarque was not convinced of his future as a writer. As he said in an interview, it did not seem possible that he could recapture that same mood again—nor did he.

Young writers feel the pull of two powerful tides in their development. The first tide which they feel in their early twenties is the urge to get away from the family, the home town, from everything that is familiar. It is nostalgic for me to remember the roll call of those who went out in the 1920's: Ernest Hemingway, who had been an ambulance driver, as I had, was called back to Europe by his love for Paris, for Spain and the brave bulls. F. Scott Fitzgerald, earning $40,000 a year, is in Paris working on his short stories. Glenway West-cott is there writing a novel about his grandmother and an apple orchard back home in Wisconsin. Archibald MacLeish, offered a partnership in the best law

firm in Boston, resigns the same day in order to go to France and free-lance as a poet. Thornton Wilder, after years of teaching in a boys' school, has cut free and is on his way to Rome to write his first novel, *The Cabala*. Kenneth Roberts, with his wife to do his typing, has taken a shipload of books about the American Revolution to a hill town in Italy where he begins the first of his big historical novels, *A Rabble in Arms*. These are just a few of those who took the gamble. Can you get a clearer view of America from the east bank of the Seine? Perhaps. You can also get privacy, stimulus, and the chance to discover on your own what you are good for.

The incoming tide, or shall we call it the homecoming, occurs at a later stage when the writer is in his early thirties, and for many this can be the experience which finally unlocks the inner door. Toward the close of her career, Willa Cather, in an essay in *The Colophon*, gave a touching account of what this homecoming had meant to her. Willa Cather was a Virginian who spent her girlhood on a farm in Nebraska. Having to support herself on her graduation from the state university, she began to teach in the public schools of Pittsburgh, and she rationed every penny against that day when she would have money enough to go abroad. At last she had enough savings for six months leave of absence in Lon-

don. There she rented a studio, made some English friends, and wrote her first novel, *Alexander's Bridge*, about some "interesting" people who got involved in a Chelsea studio. On her return, the novel was accepted and published; no one read it, and Miss Cather resumed her teaching. What follows is in her words:

When I got back to Pittsburgh I began to write a book entirely for myself; a story about some Scandinavians and Bohemians who had been neighbors of ours when I lived on a ranch in Nebraska, when I was eight or nine years old. I found it a much more absorbing occupation than writing *Alexander's Bridge*; a different process altogether. Here there was no arranging or "inventing"; everything was spontaneous and took its own place, right or wrong. This was like taking a ride through a familiar country on a horse that knew the way, on a fine morning when you felt like riding. The other was like riding in a park, with someone not altogether congenial, to whom you had to be talking all the time . . .

*O Pioneers!* interested me tremendously, because it had to do with a kind of country I loved, because it was about old neighbors, once very dear, whom I had almost forgotten in the hurry and excitement of growing up and finding out what the world was like and trying to get on in it. But I did not in the least expect that other people would see anything in a slow-moving story, without "action," without "humor," without a "hero"; a story concerned entirely with heavy farming people,

with cornfields and pasture lands and pig yards—set in Nebraska, of all places! . . .

*O Pioneers!* was not only about Nebraska farmers; the farmers were Swedes! At that time, 1912, the Swede had never appeared on the printed page in this country except in broadly humorous sketches; and the humor was based on two peculiarities; his physical strength and his inability to pronounce the letter "j."

The country Willa Cather entered in her sturdy novel, *O Pioneers!*, led, as you know, to places of even greater depth and feeling, to *My Antonia*, to *A Lost Lady*, and to *Death Comes to the Archbishop*. In short, what Willa Cather found on her homecoming to Nebraska was an American community with its loyalties and passions, so alive that it could be identified by readers in every other state. That is exactly what Sinclair Lewis found when with his somewhat disapproving New York wife he returned to Sauk Center, Minnesota; what Erskine Caldwell found on Tobacco Road; what Tom Wolfe looking back from London and Vienna saw far off in Asheville, North Carolina, the setting of *Look Homeward, Angel*. The homecoming made all the difference to John Marquand as he turned away from writing detective stories about Mr. Moto and toward Newburyport, Massachusetts, the setting for so many of his novels; just as it did to William Faulkner, returning in 1919 from the Royal Air Force to that imagined

county with its unpronounceable name—which he made his own—in Mississippi. One has to be approaching middle age to get the full, deep value of this reunion, but the experience when it comes is truly a wellspring of American literature.

I should like to conclude with some notes on loyalty. For going on four decades I have been dealing with authors young and old, and experience has taught me that the relations between author and editor are of a very sensitive tissue, and what is more, they must be expected to change from year to year. When the young author approaches a publisher with his first novel, he comes in a humble mood needing encouragement and his published work is often the better for the advice he is given. At the outset, the publisher has the authority and it is the young writer who looks for support and for guidance. But the moment the author has established his reputation and has a firm hold on a readership, this relationship is reversed. Now it is the author who has the authority and in the majority of cases he no longer needs or wants the advice which he had so eagerly awaited a few years earlier. The Thomas Wolfe who accepted so hungrily the editing which Maxwell Perkins devoted to *Look Homeward, Angel* had outgrown the need for such meticulous attention by the time he was writing *Of*

*Time and the River.* Now it was Thomas Wolfe who had the authority, and when he turned away from Perkins, it was to find another publisher who would take him on his own terms.

Sinclair Lewis, who revered Alfred Harcourt as a publisher and loved him as a friend, wrote his best novels for Harcourt, Brace and was eager to invest his small savings in that firm when it was founded, but after *Elmer Gantry* and *Dodsworth*, Lewis's expectation of what was due him went up several notches, and he began to feel that Harcourt, Brace were taking his work for granted. The advertising wasn't enough, so his letters say, and by inference neither was the publishers' solicitude.

The one thing the best writers I have known have in common is their affection, amounting at times to reverence, for the man or woman teacher who opened for each of them the horizon and the enchantment of English. Next in order of affection is the friendship which most of them hold for the editor or the publisher, or the literary agent who has been their partner. I think of F. Scott Fitzgerald and of how in his recurring crises he turned for help to his agent Harold Ober; Alfred Knopf and his encompassing friendships with Thomas Mann and Henry L. Mencken; John Marquand and Alfred McIntyre. I think of Rudyard Kipling and

of the affection which in his prickly way he bestowed on his American publisher F. N. Doubleday. Such loyalties, broken only by death, have enriched my own editing far beyond the power of the dollar: They make publishing the unique business that it is.

# ❧ INDEX

141

# Index

**143**

# Index

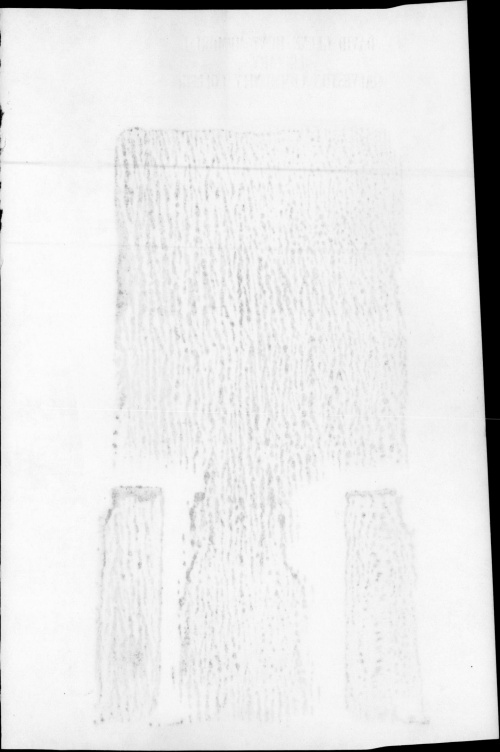